SONIA GALLICO

VATICAN

Edizioni Musei Vaticani - ATS Italia Editrice

Vatican City Today

Vatican City has an area of 44,000 hectares (440,000 square meters) and it is the smallest independent state in the world, in terms of its inhabitants and size. The borders are represented by its walls and the travertine belt that joins the two wings of the colonnade in St Peter's Square. Beyond the proper territory of the State, the Vatican jurisdiction also covers some areas in Rome and outside Rome, which enjoys the extraterritorial right.
The State of Vatican City came into existence with the Lateran Treaty between the Holy See and Italy on 11th February 1929, by which Italy recognized it as a sovereign state, constituted to give the Holy See, the supreme institution of the Catholic Church, "the absolute and visible independence; likewise to guarantee its indisputable sovereignty in international matters" as stated in the preamble of the above mentioned Treaty.
The Catholic Church carries out its evangelic mission through various particular and local Churches and through its central government, made up of the Supreme Pontiff and the Institutions, which support him in his responsibilities towards the universal Church (Holy See).
The government is an absolute monarchy. The Head of State is the Supreme Pontiff, who has complete legislative, executive and judicial powers. These powers, in periods of "Sede Vacante" (Vacancy of the Apostolic See), belong to the College of Cardinals. The legislative power is exercised by the Supreme Pontiff through a Commission made up of a Cardinal President and other Cardinals appointed for five years. The executive power is exercised in the name of the Supreme Pontiff by the President of the Commission who, in this role, is called President of the Governorate and is assisted by the General Secretary and the Vice-General Secretary.
The central Departments and Offices of the Governorate, that are the bodies through which this power is realized, depend on him. The judicial power is exercised, in the name of the Supreme Pontiff, by the constituted organs according to the juridical structure of the State.
The State of Vatican City has its own flag characterized by two fields divided vertically: a yellow one next to the flagstaff, and a white one with the Pontifical tiara and the decussate keys. It also has its own currency, now the euro, and issues its own stamps. In the Vatican City they publish a newspaper, called "L'Osservatore Romano", founded in 1861, and, since 1931 a radio network has been active, Radio Vatican, which broadcasts all over the world in various languages. Nowadays there are about 800 inhabitants, 450 of whom possess the Vatican citizenship, while the others, although living there temporarily or permanently, have not got the right to Vatican citizenship. The Pope's security is guaranteed by the Swiss Guards, founded in 1506, who wear a uniform which, according to tradition, was designed by Michelangelo, and by the Gerdarmerie, responsible for all the police and security services of the State.

St Paul's outside the Walls

St John's Lateran

St Mary Major

St Peter's Basilica

Vatican City through the centuries

The term Vatican anciently identified the marshy area on the right bank of the river Tiber, between Milvio Bridge and the present Sixtus Bridge. During the royal period and the republican age, the area was known as Ager Vaticanus and extended northwards as far as the mouth of the Cremera, and southwards at least as far as the Janiculum. In the Imperial age, from the 2nd century A.D. the toponym Vaticanum is certain and it covered an area corresponding roughly to the present Vatican City State. During the Roman period, the area outside the city of Rome was reclaimed and many villas, Agrippina's gardens –Emperor Caligula's (37-41 A.D.) mother, and wide necropolis along the main roads were built there. In his mother's gardens, Caligula built a small circus to let the charioteers train (Gaianum), restored later by Nero (54-68 A.D.), in which tradition says that Peter suffered martyrdom in the great Christian persecution ordered by Nero in 64 A.D. Various tombs have been dug along Via Trionfale, the street which from St Peter's Square leads northwards to Monte Mario, while along Via Cornelia, which led westwards, the necropolis with the tomb of the apostle Peter rose. The presence of Peter represents the topographic centre of the area as since then it has been the destination of the most significant among the Christian pilgrimages: many Christian believers, led by their desire to be near St Peter, will find their burial next to him. The necropolis was covered during the building of the basilica dedicated to the apostle, commissioned by Emperor Constantine (306-337 A.D.), which determined the following development of the area.
After formally recognizing the Christian religion with the Edict of Milan in 313 A.D., Emperor Constantine started construction on a great church around 324; it had a nave and four aisles, a transept and an apse, at the centre of which the tomb of Peter was placed. Stairs and a four-side portico for the non-baptized completed the structure. In the meantime Nero's circus was gradually falling into ruin, partly because many of its stones were used to build the new church, which was rapidly becoming a new attraction centre in Rome. Some years later, in memory of Peter, Leo IV (847-855) will build the first walls of the "civitas" which derived its name "Leonina" from him and which will be the spiritual centre of the new medieval and renaissance Rome. Although the Popes resided in the Lateran Palace, during the Middle Ages, some edifices were built in the area near St Peter's. The first of these was built under the pontificate of Eugene III (1145-1153) and Innocent III (1198-1216), and then enlarged in the late 12th-early 13th century, when the Leonine Walls were also restored. In 1309 the papal court was moved to Avignone; Rome and St Peter's were abandoned for over a century. Although the Popes returned to Rome in 1377, other fifty years passed before the city regained its former lustre. The possibility of completely rebuilding St Peter's was first broached in the mid-15th century. Pope Nicholas V (1447-1455) had the architect Bernardo Rossellino draw up plans for enlarging the Basilica, adding on an apse more prominent than the Constantinian one; after a few years, when the Turks started to advance and Constantinople fell, the project had to be abandoned. Between 1477 and 1480 Pope Sixtus IV (1471-1492) started building a great chapel, named "Sistina" after him, decorated with frescoes painted by the major Italian painters of the time. It was inaugurated on 15th August 1483. Great changes were realized by Julius II (1503-1513), who radically transformed the small city: he started pulling down the Constantinian Basilica, started the work for the new Saint Peter's, and built the famous Belvedere Courtyard to connect the small Palace of Belvedere of his predecessor Innocent VIII (1484-1492) at the north, with the cluster of the medieval buildings at the south; he also summoned Raphael and Michelangelo to Rome, asking them respectively to fresco the papal apartments and the Sistine Chapel. Work continued throughout the century: the Basilica of Saint Peter, after various vicissitudes, was planned and built by Michelangelo (mid-16th century); Giacomo Della Porta then covered the area with a magnificent "vaulted" dome. Early in the 17th century the church was enlarged by Maderno, who added two bays to the longitudinal section, and Bernini completed it in mid-century, designing the splendid square, enclosed by two hemicycles of four rows of columns, which gave it the present baroque appearance, and connected this place of prayer to the rest of the city.

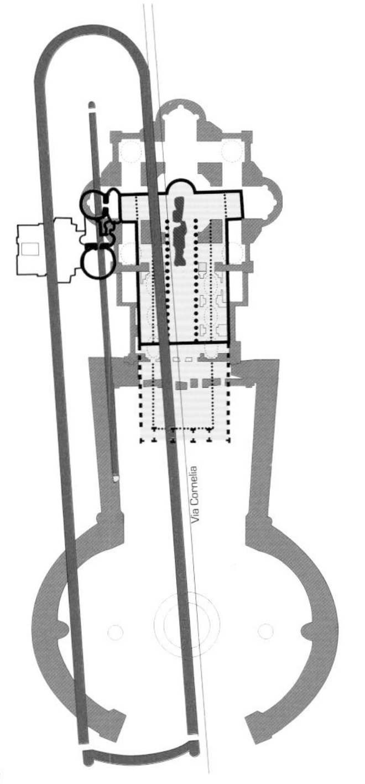

- Nero's Circus
- Pagan Necropolis
- Constantine's Basilica
- Present Basilica

History of Saint Peter's Basilica

During Nero's great Christian persecution in 64 A.D., which took place in Caligula's circus, Saint Peter was also martyred, crucified and buried there, as you can read in the Liber Pontificalis (I, 118): "via Aurelia (...) iuxta palatium Neronianum, in Vaticanum" (In the Vatican, in Via Aurelia opposite Nero's Palace). Among those who witnessed the place of the martyrdom, Eusebius of Caesarea (4th century) quotes a letter written by Gaius to Proclus, in which the presbyter invites his friend to Rome: "in the Vatican and in Via Ostiense, you will find the trophies of those who founded this Church". For this important evidence, the 2nd century aedicule, found during the excavations in the Vatican necropolis, which was to protect Saint Peter's shrine, was called "Gaius's Trophy". After Constantine's Edict of Milan (313 A.D.) the Christians could build their places of worship: Constantine himself started the building of the Basilica in 324, which had to enclose the "Gaius's Trophy" and allow Peter's tomb to become the centre of the structure. Consecrated in 329, the great basilica appeared as a longitudinal plan building with a nave, four aisles and a transept. Outside, a staircase led to the four-sided portico in front of the Basilica, known also as Paradise, with a fountain in the middle for the ablutions of the catechumens, identified with the great bronze Pinecone, mentioned also by Dante in the Divine Comedy ("and his face seemed to me long and broad / as the pinecone of Saint Peter's in Rome" Hell 31, 58-60) and today placed in the homonymous Courtyard of the Vatican Museums. Charlemagne, king of the Franks, was crowned emperor of the Holy Roman Empire in this Basilica, on Christmas eve of the year 800; pilgrims gathered to this basilica from the early 14th century coming on foot from all over Europe to worship the tomb of the "Prince of the Apostles".

When the Popes abandoned Rome during the Avignone schism (1309-1377), the basilica, which was one thousand years old by then, began to have more and more static and preservation problems. Although we have little information about this, we know for a fact that in the mid 15th century, Nicholas V asked the architect Bernardo Rossellino to draw up a project for a new choir, outside the Constantinian apse: it was actually built to the height of about 1.5 metre.

By the early 16th century the need to choose between restoring St Peter's or rebuilding it completely was imperative, so much so that the new Pope Julius II, elected in October 1503, decided to entrust this task to Donato Bramante in 1505, one of the greatest architects of his time, who was already in Rome: later on he was known as a "destroying master" for this enterprise.

There are many of Bramante's drawings in the Uffizi Gallery in Florence. All of them have a feature in common: a square plan with a Greek cross and four prominent apses; the square forms a cubical space and is covered in the centre by a hemispheric dome. As observed by A. Bruschi (1984), the structure has a precise symbolism, which can be "schematised – according to an ancient, mostly Byzantine tradition – as a cube (the world) with four extending arms (the four parts of the world), and a dome above it (heaven)".

The first pylon was started with a great ceremony on 18th April 1506, and foundations for the other three pylons were laid in the following year. Construction stopped, however, when Julius II (1513) and Bramante (1514) died; by then it had reached the top of the four pylons.

Several other proposals for St Peter's were drawn up during the next 40 years, with an animated debate going on about whether the new St Peter's should have a central or longitudinal plan. Bramante and Renaissance architects in general preferred the central plan, but the longitudinal plan or Latin cross was more in the ecclesiastic tradition and would also cover the whole sacred area of the ancient Constantinian Basilica. As the four central pylons had already been built, Raphael (1514) and Antonio da Sangallo the Younger (1538) proposed a longitudinal plan; Baldassarre Peruzzi (1520) a central plan.

Finally in 1547 Pope Paul III commissioned a new project to Michelangelo. His solution was to keep Bramante's original plan, thickening the pilasters and the external walls and creating niches and ledges by chiselling out the walls.
A vast dome was to cover the central area, where the papal altar was to be placed. This building was finally finished, although the dome had not been completed at Michelangelo's death in 1564 and his pupil Giacomo della Porta finished building it, adding a few changes, such as raising the curve of the calotte.
The dilemma regarding a central plan versus a longitudinal one had not been definitely solved, however. The Council of Trent, which ended in 1563, expressed a preference for longitudinal churches. Carlo Maderno was therefore asked to extend Michelangelo's original plan.
He achieved this by adding two bays, turning St Peter's floor plan into a Latin cross. Maderno also designed St Peter's "classical" façade, built between 1607 and 1612: unfortunately it tended to hide Michelangelo's dome and reduce its visual impact. Bernini's square tried to solve the problem with an optical effect that draws the dome forward.

History of the Fabbrica di San Pietro

The origin of the Fabbrica di San Pietro dates back to Pope Julius II, who started building the new Vatican Basilica in 1506. In 1523 Pope Clement VII appointed a permanent committee of 60 experts, who had to report directly to the Holy See and were responsible for building and administering the basilica.
In 1589 Pope Sixtus V put the committee under the authority of St Peter's Cardinal Archpriest and some years later, during the pontificate of Clement VIII (1592-1605), the committee became an independent administration called the "Congregazione della Reverenda Fabbrica di San Pietro", which inherited all the committees privileges. The prefect of this Congregation, which was composed of cardinals and prelates, was the Basilica's Cardinal Archpriest. It had the faculty of nominating its own representatives throughout the provinces of the Papal State, known as commissioners of the Reverenda Fabbrica, who were appointed annually. They had their own jurisdiction and were authorized to judge every kind of petition; moreover their decrees could be appealed in front of the Congregation.
In 1863, during the pontificate of Pius IX, the "Congregazione della Reverenda Fabbrica di San Pietro" was no longer permitted to resolve legal disputes, which were transferred to the Congregation of the Council.
After Pius X's reform in 1908, the Congregation dealt exclusively with managing the Fabbrica and, after Pope Paul VI reformed the Roman Curia in 1967, it was abolished, becoming one of the Palatine Administrations.
In the 1988 Apostolic Constitution "Pastor Bonus", Pope John Paul II established that "the Fabbrica di San Pietro, according to its laws, would continue to manage all aspects of the Basilica of the Prince of Apostles, including both the conservation and decorum of the building and the organization of the attendants and of the pilgrims who visit the temple".

IN HONOREM PRINCIPIS APOST PAVLVS V BVRGHESIVS ROMANVS PONT MAX AN MDCXII PONT VII

Saint Peter's Basilica

The Constantinian basilica disappeared with time. From the early decision of Nicholas V Parentucelli to enlarge and restore the ancient basilica, commissioning Rossellino in the second half of the 15th century, to the final realization of the building, with the façade (1612), passed just over 150 years. Quite a long period of time if you consider the number of years, but it is absolutely understandable if you think of the great amount of work and the continuous changes in the planning.
Studying the genesis of Saint Peter's Basilica means studying the history of the evolution of the thought and art in the various historic periods.
In the over 150 years needed to complete the Basilica, the most famous artists of the time directed the "Fabbrica di San Pietro": Raphael Sanzio, who decided to transform Bramante's Greek cross building in a Latin cross one in 1514, Antonio da Sangallo the Younger and Michelangelo who, under the pontificate of Paul III decided to reuse the original Greek cross plan, designed the dome and followed its realization until his death in 1564.
During the following thirty years, the "Fabbrica di San Pietro" was directed by Vignola and followed by the architects Giacomo Della Porta and Domenico Fontana, who completed Michelangelo's plan of the dome around 1588.
Saint Peter's Basilica reached its present appearance thanks to Carlo Maderno, who went back to the Latin cross plan and defined the scenographic aspect of the façade.
The work on the basilica was completed under the pontificate of Urban VIII in 1626, but it was only between 1656 and 1667 that Bernini, commissioned by Alexander VII, planned and realized the great colonnade in Saint Peter's Square with the 1st century B.C. obelisk in the middle. Originally set in the centre of Caligula's circus where Saint Peter was martyred, it was moved to the present site in 1585 by Domenico Fontana, commissioned by Sixtus V.
Saint Peter's Basilica can host 20,0000 believers; it is 190 m long, the aisles are 58 m wide, the nave is 45.50 m high as far as the vault, the dome is about 136 m high as far as the cross; the interiors, characterized by huge mosaics, are the precious sites for some of the most famous art works all over the world, for example Bernini's Baldachin and Michelangelo's Pietà.

The Square

Realized by Bernini between 1656 and 1667, during the pontificate of Alexander VII (1655-1667), the square is made up of two different areas. The first has a trapezoid shape, marked by two straight closed and convergent arms which side the church square. The second area is elliptic and is surrounded by the two hemicycles of a four-row colonnade, because, as Bernini said: "considering that Saint Peter's is almost the matrix of all the churches, its portico had to give an open-armed maternal welcome to all Catholics confirming their faith, to Heretics rejoining them with the Church and to the Infidels, enlightening them about the true faith".
Bernini had in fact designed a three-armed portico, but after Alexander VII's death construction on the portico stopped and the third arm was never built. It would have enclosed the whole building and separated the ellipse from the quarter of Borgo, thus creating a "surprise effect" for the pilgrim who suddenly found himself in the square. This effect was somewhat achieved by the buildings surrounding the square, the so-called "Spina di Borgo", which naturally "closed in" the square. In 1950, Via della Conciliazione, a

new, wide street leading to the Vatican Basilica, was opened on the place of Spina di Borgo. It exalts the majestic view of Saint Peter's dome, but it had also deeply modified Bernini's original plan. The measurements of the square are impressive: it is 320 m deep, its diameter is 240 m and it is surrounded by 284 columns, set out in rows of four and 88 pilasters. Along the balustrade, on the columns, Bernini's pupils realized 140 statues of Saints, 3.20 m high, around 1670. The obelisk, moved in the middle of the square by Domenico Fontana in 1585, is sided by two great fountains made by Bernini (1675) and Maderno (1614).
Below, at the foot of the staircase, the statues of Saint Peter and Saint Paul seem to welcome the Catholics.
Of great interest is the Royal Staircase, which links the square to the Vatican Palaces and considered by Bernini himself "... the least bad thing he had ever made". Realized between 1662 and 1666, and though it actually measures 60 metres, perspective devices, like a progressive narrowing of the width and a reduced distance between the columns towards the top, make it look much longer.

The Dome

The dome was designed by Michelangelo, who worked on the construction of the basilica from 1547. By the end of his long life (he died at 89 in 1564) construction had reached the drum of the dome, which alternates highly prominent double columns with gabled windows. Then, Giacomo Della Porta, Michelangelo's pupil, took over the direction of the work, raising the vault of the dome about 7 metres and completing it in 1590 in just 22 months, under the pontificate of Pope Sixtus V.
The dome has a double calotte, with an inner diameter of 42.56 metres and it measures 136.57 metres from the base to the top of the cross; the lantern is 17 metres high.
This dome was used as a model for other domes in the western world: among which, although realized with different techniques, the dome of Saint Paul's in London (1675), that of the Les Invalides in Paris (1680-1691) and the neo-classical dome of the Capital in Washington (1794-1817).

The Façade

Designed by the architect Carlo Maderno, it was completed in 1614. It is 114.69 metres wide and 48 metres high, and has an order of Corinthian columns and pilasters, over which lies an imposing cornice with central tympanum, crowned by a balustrade with thirteen statues (nearly 6 metres high) with the statue of the blessing Saviour in the middle.

An inscription on the entablature commemorates the fact that the façade was built during the pontificate of Pope Paul V (1605-1621) Borghese.

In the lower order there are five entrances to the atrium, over which are nine windows, three of which have a balcony. The central window is the so-called "Benediction Loggia", where the Pope gives his first blessing "urbi et orbi" (to the city and to the world) upon his election and at Christmas and Easter.

The restoration which ended in July 1999, aimed at bringing out some whitewashes realized by Maderno, hidden under the patina of time.

PAVLVS V PONT MAX AN

Holy Door

Interior of the Basilica

The atrium (corresponding to the ancient portico of the early Christian basilicas) is considered one of the most remarkable works of Carlo Maderno and was realized between 1608 and 1612.
The central door is by the Florentine sculptor Antonio Averulino, known as Filarete; it dates from 1455 and comes from the ancient Constantinian church. Saint Peter and Saint Paul are represented here with scenes from their martyrdom.
The Holy Door is on the right, cast in bronze by the sculptor Vico Consorti in 1950. This door is opened and closed in the Pope's presence at every Jubilee Year.
On the far left of the vestibule is the equestrian statue of Charlemagne, made by Agostino Cornacchini (1725); on the

Atrium
of the Vatican Basilica

NI CAELORVM TV ES PETRVS
FIDES
MVNDO

Gian Lorenzo Bernini,
Bronze Baldachin

right vestibule is Bernini's equestrian statue of the Emperor Constantine (1670).

The Latin cross structure of the interior dates back to the early 1600 and was realized by Maderno, who completed the basilica and realized the three bays of the nave and the two aisles, forming a whole with the Michelangelesque central octagon. It is an immense and magnificent space, richly decorated with Baroque stuccos, mosaics and statues, almost overwhelming at first glance. The visitor usually needs to pause for a moment before he can take in its vast size and just comparing the height of the holy-water fonts and their supporting puttos with that of the people around them he can have an idea of the church's proportions.

The basilica is 187 metres long, 58 metres wide across the aisles and 140 metres wide at the transept: the maximum height of the vault in the nave is 46 metres (as high as a 15 storey building!).

Nave

The visitor should first walk down the nave, noting the marks on the floor with the comparative lengths of the biggest churches in the world; then he can go back to the aisle near the entrance door,

Michelangelo,
Pietà

Michelangelo,
Pietà, detail

following the numbering on the plan (see page 154).
The nave has huge, fluted and cabled pilasters (the lower part of the fluting is full); each one has niches with 39 statues of saints who founded the various religious orders and congregations. The vault was decorated with gold stuccos in 1780, under Pius VI.
The right aisle, looking at the altar, contains many great artistic and religious works. Michelangelo's Pietà is in the first chapel, shielded by thick glass: this masterpiece dates from 1499, when the artist was only 24 years old.
The Madonna's youthful, sweet face expresses her submission to destiny, as she cradles the dead Christ's limp body in her lap; yet the rich drapery of her dress and veil suggest an extraordinary physical and moral strength, which contrasts with the delicate, 15th century features. This is the only work signed by the artist on the belt.
The Chapel of the Most Holy Sacrament comes next, with a tabernacle on the altar resembling Bramante's Tempietto at Saint Peter's in Montorio, on the Janiculum Hill. Bernini sculptured this gilded bronze tabernacle in 1674; two kneeling angels were added to it later on.
At the end of the right aisle is the famous Monument to Gregory XIII (1572-1585), completed by the sculptor Camillo Rusconi in 1723,

Bronze Statue
of St Peter

with allegorical figures of Religion and Fortitude and a dragon, the heraldic symbol of the pope's family, below the sarcophagus.
Returning to the nave, one can see the famous statue of Saint Peter Enthroned, which most critics attributed to Arnolfo di Cambio (1245-1302); some scholars, however, date the statue to the 5th century.
One foot has been almost completely worn away by the faithful, who kiss it to show their devotion to the Saint.
Four huge, square pilasters mark where the longitudinal nave and transept meet; niches have been carved out of the pilasters' oblique walls, containing four colossal statues which embody crucial moments of Christ's passion: St Longinus, the soldier who pierced Christ's side with his spear and later converted to Christianity, executed by Bernini in 1638; St Helen, Emperor Constantine's mother, who brought the cross and nails of Christ's martyrdom to Rome; St Veronica, who wiped Christ's face with a cloth on the road

Saint Longinus

Saint Helen

Saint Veronica

Saint Andrew

Gian Lorenzo Bernini,
Altar of the Cathedra,
detail

Interior of the Dome

to Calvary; St Andrew, Peter's brother, who was crucified in Greece. The latter three statues are by Bernini's pupils.
The papal altar in the middle of the church is surmounted by the famous gilded bronze Baldachin, designed by a youthful Bernini between 1624 and 1632.
It is 29 metres high and was commissioned by pope Urban VIII Barberini (1623-1644) to fill the "empty" space below the dome and create an upward movement.
The bronze used for the baldachin probably comes from the Pantheon's pronaos, and this gives rise to a saying, "quod non fecerunt barbari fecerunt Barberini" ("what the Barbarians didn't do, was done by the Barberini"). The baldachin has four colossal, twisted columns, splendidly fluted and decorated with olive and laurel branches, ending in a composite capital. The covering has extremely elegant volutes and statues on each corner, and is crowned by a gilded bronze sphere. Note the tassels with bees (an emblem of the Barberini family, symbolizing their industriousness), which almost seem to rustle in an imaginary wind. A gold dove inside represents the Holy Spirit.

Detail of
the Confession

Underneath this structure is the “Tomb of Saint Peter”, where, according to tradition, the remains of the Apostle are kept, making it one of the places most venerated by Christians and the best place to build the most important Christian temple. Recent archaeological evidences seem to confirm this tradition.

Above the Baldachin is the majestic dome (see page 14), with paintings on the inside realized after cartoons by Giuseppe Cesari, known as Cavalier d’Arpino, between 1603 and 1613. Along the base is a gold inscription in Latin, which reads: “You are Peter and on this rock I will build my Church, and I will give you the keys to Heaven”.

The Monument to Clement XIII (1758-1769) in the right-hand transept also deserves attention. It was built in 1784 by the greatest Italian neo-classical sculptor, Antonio Canova. It was

Antonio Canova,
Monument
to Clement XIII

commissioned in 1784 and was built using Bernini's tombs as a model, with a portrait of the Pope above the sarcophagus, flanked by two allegorical figures: Religion with a cross in its hand and the Spirit of death, putting out the fire of life. Two lions watch over the tomb in turn. St Peter's Cathedra is one of Bernini's sculptural masterpieces. Inside the great oval window, shielded by a thin sheet of alabaster, with some rays, which divide the surface into twelve sectors symbolizing the Apostles, is the Holy Spirit, portrayed as a dove. Around it, an extraordinary cloud of angels and puttos surmount St Peter's bronze Cathedra.

Inside the Cathedra is a wooden throne, which, according to tradition, was used by the first Apostle, but actually it was a gift from Charles the Bald to the Pope in 875. It is flanked by St Ambrose and St Augustine, fathers of the Latin Church, and St Athanasius with St John Chrysostom, fathers of the Greek Church. The work was

Gian Lorenzo Bernini,
Monument
to Alexander VII

Antonio Canova, Monument to the Stuarts

finished in 1666, under the Pope Alexander VII.
On either side of the cathedra are the monuments to Paul III by Guglielmo della Porta (left), and to Urban VIII by Bernini (right).
Another artistically relevant sculpture is Bernini's last work: the Monument to Alexander VII in the left transept, commissioned by the pope himself when the artist was eighty years old. The skeleton, below the red drapery and the hourglass symbolize the passing of time and the inevitability of death.
Along the left aisle is Antonio Canova's monument to the Stuarts (1819), dedicated to the last descendents of the courageous English family, portrayed in profile below the bracket.
The monument to Pope John XXIII (1958-63) is by the sculptor Emilio Greco (1964-1967).

Antonio del Pollaiolo,
Monument
to Sixtus IV

Historical Artistic Museum - Saint Peter's Treasury

After passing through the common Sacristy, a central plan area of the late 18th century, built with columns from Villa Adriana in Tivoli, one enters St Peter's Treasury, which contains church ornaments, statues, papal mitres and various objects, usually gifts of kings or princes. Notable pieces include the Monument to Sixtus IV (1471-1484), a work by Antonio del Pollaiolo, a 15th century Florentine artist: the sarcophagus shows the Pope surrounded by the virtues and liberal arts. Cardinal Giuliano della Rovere, the Pope-to-be Julius II, commissioned it in 1493.

Vatican Grottos

Vatican Grottos

Positioned just below the church and above Constantine's 4th century basilica, the Grottos contain chapels dedicated to various saints and tombs of kings, queens and popes from the 10th century onwards. The holiest place is Peter's tomb, containing the aedicule, built in the 4th century by the Emperor Constantine, on the spot were the Apostle's tomb was thought to be. In one of the chapels around the apse is a fresco by the 14th century Roman painter Pietro Cavallini: it is the "Madonna della Bocciata", because of Mary's swollen face. According to an old legend, her face bled because a drunken soldier had thrown a bowl into the holy image, after he had lost at a game of bowls. The Monuments to Paul VI (1978) and Pope John Paul II (2005) are also in the Grottos.

Pre-Constantinian Necropolis

Excavations held around 1940 brought to light various tombs from the 1st century B.C., originally in the northern end of Nero's Circus. They were richly decorated and frescoed pagan tombs, later flanked by Christian tombs, which were sometimes very poor. At the end of the necropolis is an aedicule, which, both legend and recent studies indicate as the Apostle Peter's tomb.

Vatican Palaces

As early as the mid 9th century there was a small fortified city in the area around ancient St Peter's Basilica, surrounded by walls built by Leo IV (847-855), the so-called "Leonine city". Between the end of the 13th and the first decades of the 14th century, some edifices were built around the square courtyard, known as "Pappagallo": they were the first Vatican Palaces.
After the Avignon Schism (1309-1377), no new buildings went up until the end of the 15th century, when the Palaces of Sixtus IV (1471-1484) were built; these include the Sistine Chapel, which takes its name from the Pope. Innocent VIII (1484-1492) also built some palaces, about 300 metres north of the Vatican Basilica.
Julius II (1503-1513) and his architect, Donato Bramante, had the idea of joining the two groups of buildings constructed by his predecessors, adding two magnificent, three-level courtyards. During the 16th and 17th centuries popes continued to work on and enlarge the Vatican palaces. Sixtus V (1585-1590) also built the palace where the present pope lives and where every Sunday at noon he stands at the window (the second from the right on the third floor), and blesses the crowd who gathers in the magnificent Vatican square.

RAFFAELLO
PERUGINO
GIOTTO
VIALE

Vatican Museums,
Pinacoteca,
prospect of the
Square Garden

MVSEI VATICANI

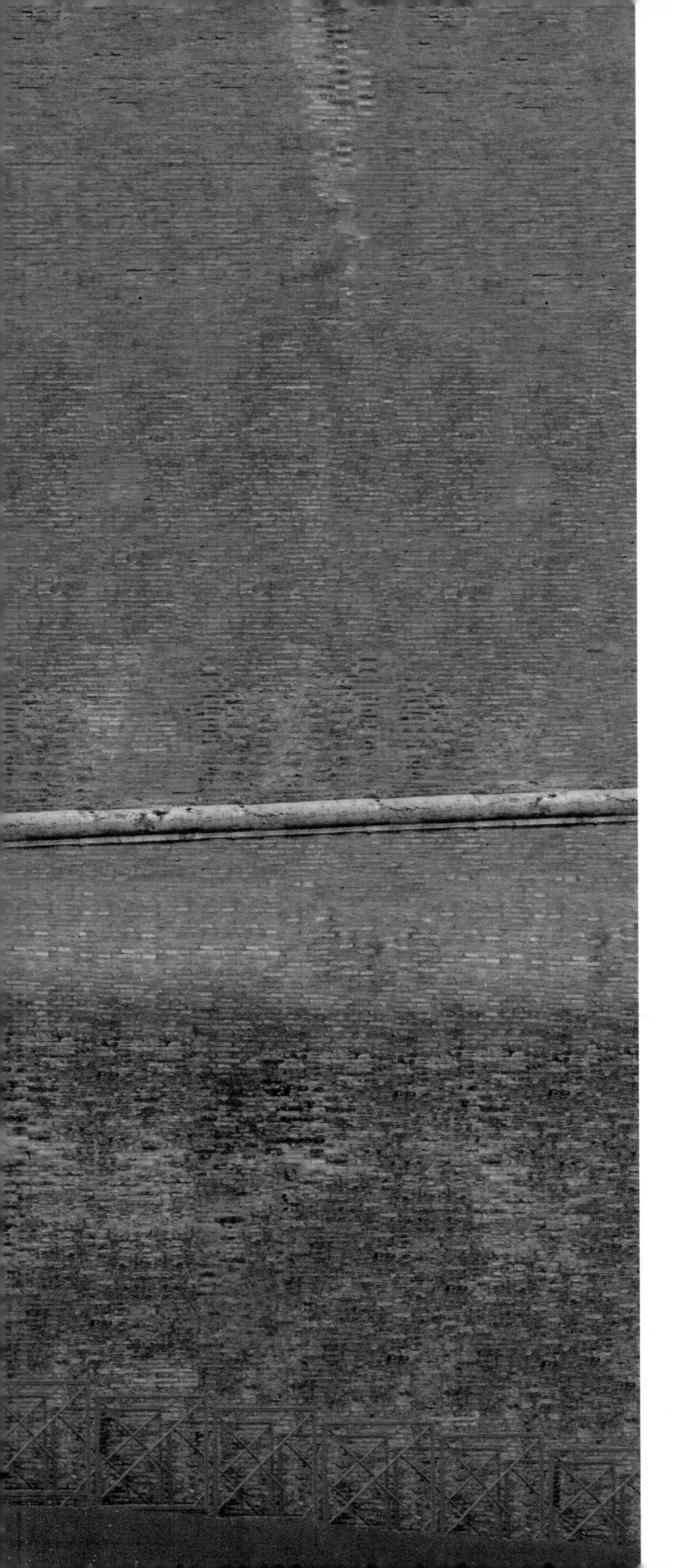

Vatican Museums

The collections in the Vatican Museums were built up gradually, in spite of wars, destruction and thefts, by various popes from Renaissance onwards: now they constitute one of the biggest museum complexes in the world. In this text, the following areas will be described: the Pinacoteca (Picture Gallery), Pius-Clementine Museum, Raphael's Rooms and the Sistine Chapel.

Old Entrance to the Vatican Museums, Monumental Door surmounted by the coat-of-arms of Pope Pius XI, sided by the statues representing Michelangelo and Raphael

Room II - Giotto,
Stefaneschi Triptych,
verso

Pinacoteca

The building of the Pinacoteca, completed in 1931, was commissioned by Pius IX (1922 -1939), expressly to house a collection of paintings, belonging to various popes and started by Pius VI (1775-1799). Many of the paintings on exhibit were taken to Paris by Napoleon in 1797, but returned to Italy after the Congress of Vienna (1815), thanks also to the intercession of the sculptor Antonio Canova. The works, covering a period from the Middle Ages to 1800, are set in chronological order, in eighteen rooms.
- **Room I** – contains collections by painters of the 12th, 13th and 14th centuries, known as "primitives", because they pre-date Giotto. The paintings on wood are generally characterized by golden background, figures with clear outlines and not shaded colours and a lack of perspective in the architectonic elements. The main figure is often shown in the middle of the painting, while scenes from his life are on the sides.
- **Room II** – dedicated to the 14th century painters from Siena and to Giotto (1267-1337), the greatest Italian painter in the Middle Ages. Noteworthy are: "Christ before Pilate" by Pietro

Room I – Nicholas and John,
The Last Judgement,
detail

Room II – Lippo d'Andrea, Nativity of Christ

Lorenzetti (1280/1285-1348), where his highly refined and elegant painting, typical of the Siena painters, is shown in sinuous forms and warm colours; " the Redeemer conferring a blessing" by Simone Martini (1284-1344). Giotto's "Triptych", known as "Stefaneschi", named after the client, is in the middle of the room. It is painted on both sides: the central panel represents Saint Peter enthroned with angels and offerers on the recto and Christ enthroned with angels and offerer (Cardinal Stefaneschi) on the verso. Noteworthy are the refined mosaic decorations on the throne.

- **Room III** – shows works of the early 15th century, when a new painting style was taking hold in Florence: the golden background was slowly disappearing, figures were becoming more solid, the central perspective was the only vanishing point giving depth.

The "Madonna and Child, with St Dominic and St Catherine", a small tempera painting on wood by Fra Angelico, a Dominican monk, is remarkably beautiful. It is a perfect blend of the new painting theories with a typically Mediaeval love for miniatures.

- **Room IV** – contains works by the painter from Emilia, Melozzo da Forlì (1438-1494): the "Musician Angels" are fragments from a huge fresco, "Christ in Glory between Angels and Apostles", which covered the apsidal conch of the Church of Sts Apostles, near Venice Square: the daringly foreshortened figures, serene faces and light hair are often reproduced in musical history books.

Room II – Gentile da Fabriano,
Stories of St Nicholas of Bari,
The Saint saves a ship from sinking

Room II – School of the Marches,
Nativity and Announcement
of the Magi,
detail

Room III – Fra Angelico,
Stories of St Nicholas of Bari:
Birth of the Saint,
His Vocation,
The Gift to the three poor girls

Room III – Fra Angelico,
Madonna and Child with
Sts Dominic and
Catherine of Alexandria

Room III – Filippo Lippi
and assistants,
Crowning of the Virgin

Room IV – Melozzo da Forlì,
Angel playing the lute

Room IV – Melozzo da Forlì,
Sixtus IV and Platina

Room VI – Niccolò di Liberatore,
Crowning of the Virgin,
Burial of Christ and Saints

Another "taken" fresco is "Sixtus IV and Platina" (1477), by Melozzo: it represents Platina being appointed prefect of the Apostolic Library and Giuliano della Rovere, pope-to-be Julius II, wearing a cardinal habit. All the characters are rigorously set in perspective architecture, with typical coffered ceilings with rosettes, golden moulding and oak garlands (Sixtus IV also belonged to the della Rovere family).

- **Room V** – is dedicated to 15th century painting. In the painting "Miracles of Saint Vincenzo Ferrer" by Ercole de' Roberti (c. 1450-1496), a theme typical of Italian painting during that period can be seen: a taste for ancient ruins and past architectures.
- **Room VI** – contains polyptychs by 15th century artists, often with 14th century features (golden background, taste for details, etc.).
- **Room VII** – has paintings of the Umbrian school, including "Madonna and Child with four Saints" by Perugino (1446-1524), completed in 1495, where the calm, balanced figures are framed by architecture set in a gentle, serene landscape. The artist had already painted the "Handing over of the Keys" in the Sistine Chapel (1461). Noteworthy is the "Saint Jerome Enthroned" by Giovanni Santi (? -1494), the great Raphael's father.
- **Room VIII** – shows a tapestry of the Last Supper, taken from the work

Room VII – Perugino,
Madonna and Child
with four Saints

Room VII – Umbrian School,
Madonna and Child with
St John the Infant

Room VIII – Raphael,
Transfiguration

Room VIII – Raphael,
Madonna of Foligno

Room IX – Leonardo, St Jerome

of Leonardo da Vinci (1452-1519) and 16th century Flemish tapestries made using cartoons by Raphael (1483-1520): the latter was set on the lower part of the walls in the Sistine Chapel. In the middle of the room are paintings by Raphael: on the right is the "Crowning of the Virgin" of 1502-1503, a youthful work; on the left, the "Madonna of Foligno" (1511-1512) from the same period as the works in Julius II's Apartment, known as the "Stanze"; in the centre is the "Transfiguration" (1518-1520), a masterpiece in oil on wood, where the dramatic figures show how the artist was influenced by Michelangelo[1].

- **Room IX** – contains Leonardo's famous "St Jerome", an unfinished work dated 1482. The landscape on the upper left is typically Leonardesque, with glaciers and remote mountains, as is the gaunt figure of the saint, who abandoned all his worldly goods and became ascetic. The "Lament over the dead Christ" by Venetian Giovanni Bellini (1430-1516) is also in the room.

- **Room X** – contains works by some of the greatest Venetian painters of the 16th century; the "Madonna of St Niccolò dei Frari" with the

[1] Raphael and Michelangelo had worked in Rome between 1508 and 1512, summoned by Pope Julius II to work respectively on the Rooms and the Sistine Chapel. The artist from Urbino died suddenly in April 1520.

beautiful veiled woman on the right is by Titian (1490-1576), while a painting representing Saint Helen is by Paolo Caliari, known as il Veronese (1528-1588): the saint is seen from below and is portrayed in the artist's typical fashion, like a wealthy woman wearing a wide glimmering brocade gown.

- **Room XI** – has works by painters of the second half of the 16th century, including the "Lapidation of Saint Stephen" by Giorgio Vasari (1511-74), the "Sacrifice of Isaac" by Ludovico Carracci, the "Annunciation" by Cavalier d'Arpino, dated 1606, and "Rest during the Flight into Egypt" by Barocci (1528-1612).
- **Room XII** – is dedicated to early 17th century painters, who inherited a taste for realism and daring perspective from Caravaggio.

Room X – Veronese, Saint Helen

Room X – Paris Bordon, St George killing the Dragon

Room XI – Federico Barocci,
Rest during the
Flight into Egypt

Room XII – Guido Reni,
St Matthew and the Angel

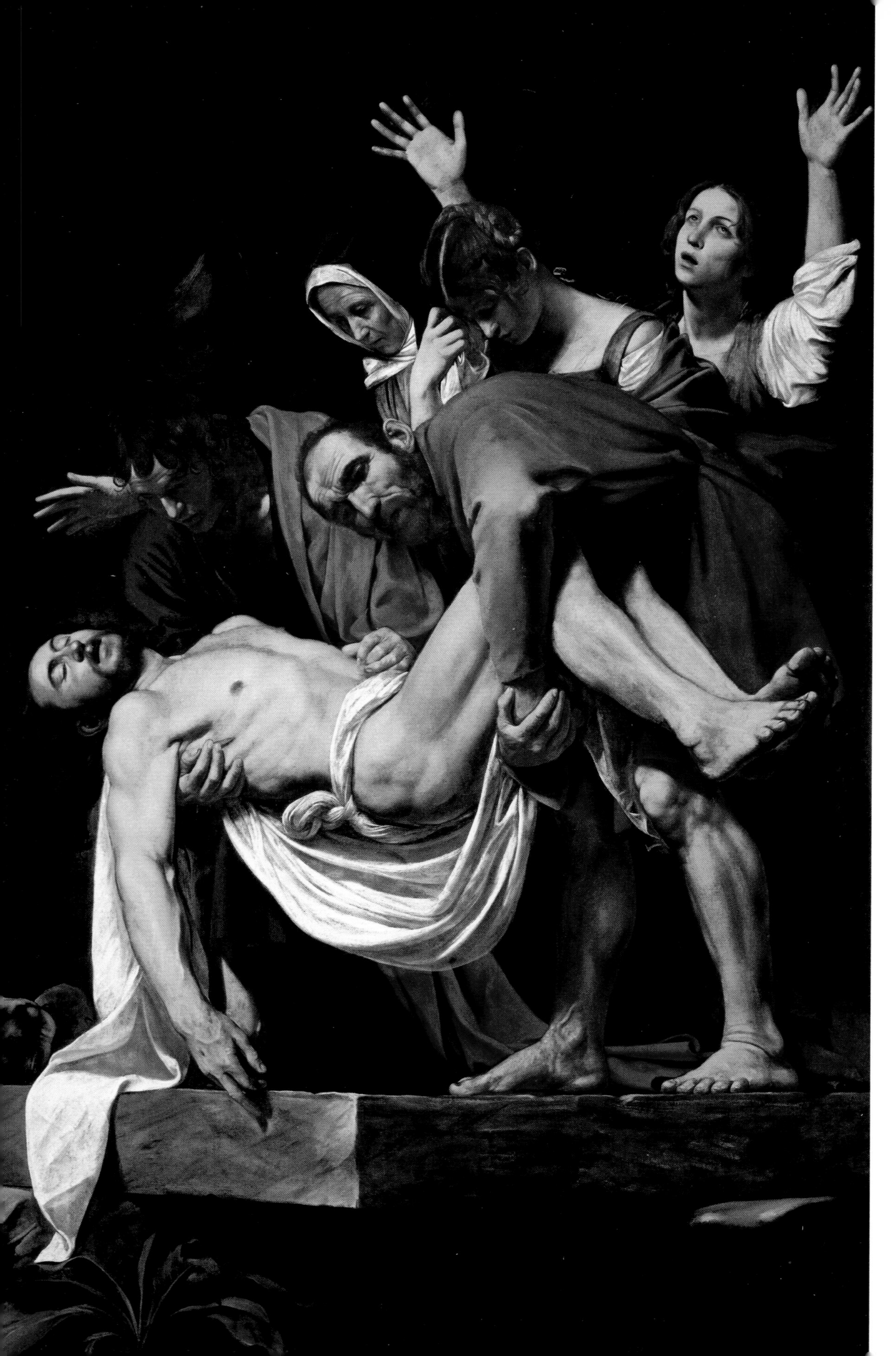

Room XII – Caravaggio,
Deposition from the Cross

Room XIII – Guido Reni,
Fortune restrained by Love

Room XIII
Pietro da Cortona,
David killing
the giant Goliath

Of remarkable interest is the "Communion of Saint Jerome" painted by Domenichino in 1616, the "Crucifixion of Saint Peter" and "Saint Matthew and the Angel" by Guido Reni (1575-1642), "Saint Peter Disclaiming Christ" by the Caravaggio school, "Deposition from the Cross" by Caravaggio dated 1604 and the "Martyrdom of Saint Erasmus" by the French painter Nicolas Poussin.

- **Room XIII, XIV and XV** – the first room contains paintings by the

Room XV – Francesco Mancini,
Rest during the Flight into Egypt

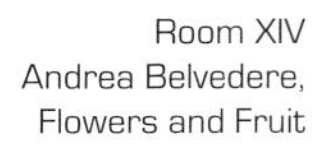

Room XIV
Andrea Belvedere,
Flowers and Fruit

Room XIV – Pietro Navarra, Still life with classical elements and fruit

Flemish Van Dyck, the Italian Pietro da Cortona and the French Nicolas Poussin, while rooms XIV and XV has "genre" paintings of the 17th and 18th centuries.

- **Room XVI** – contains paintings by Wenzel Peter (1745-1829), a Bohemian painter born near Prague: note the superb "Adam and Eve in the Garden of Eden", with an exceptional variety of flowers and animals. In the two nearby small rooms are some clay models of Gian Lorenzo Bernini statues, realized for the works in Saint Peter's Basilica (Room XVII) and some 15th to 19th century Greek icons (Room XVIII).

Room XVI – Wenzel Peter,
Adam and Eve in
the Garden of Eden

Courtyard of the "Pigna",
Arnaldo Pomodoro,
Sphere with Sphere

Vatican Courtyards

After passing the Atrium of the "Corazze" on the left, and crossing the Atrium with its Four Gates, the visitor enters the Courtyard of the "Pigna", created from the 16th century area of the "Belvedere". Donato Bramante was asked to design the Courtyard of the "Belvedere" by Julius II in 1506, to connect the Palace of Innocent VIII (1484-1492) with the Sistine Chapel, built by Sixtus IV (1471-1484). Originally the Courtyard was on three levels, joined by elegant stairways and flanked by galleries characterized by pilasters surmounted by broad arches. Both the paving and the galleries were slightly angled towards the Sistine Chapel, so that from the papal apartments the courtyard looked even bigger than it actually was.
A large niche, planned at its northern end to complete the perspective, was realized, as it can now be seen in the so-called Courtyard of the "Pigna", by architect Pirro Ligorio in 1565, using the Pantheon dome as a model. The picturesque prints from the early 16th century give an idea of the festivals and carousels that used to take place there. The Courtyard of the "Belvedere" was divided into two parts at the end of the 16th century, when Sixtus V (1585-1590) built a wing of the Library across it. Another transversal building was added in 1822, called the "Braccio Nuovo", intended for a collection of statues (see page 68).
There are now three courtyards in the area: the Courtyard of the "Pigna", the Library Courtyard and the Courtyard of the "Belvedere".
The Courtyard of the "Pigna" is named after a colossal bronze pinecone, almost 4 metres high, which, in the classic age, stood near the Pantheon in Rome, known as the "Pigna quarter"; it was probably first moved to the atrium of the ancient St Peter's Basilica during the Middle Ages and then moved here in 1608. Two bronze peacocks, copies of 2nd century A.D. originals in the Braccio Nuovo, flank the pinecone.
In the middle of the wide-open space are two concentric spheres by sculptor Arnaldo Pomodoro (1990).

Commemorative Stelae
of Queen Hatshepsut

Egyptian Museum

The Egyptian Museum is reached by the Simonetti Staircase, named after the builder who planned it between 1771 and 1784. It was founded in 1839 by Gregory XVI and contains both Egyptian findings bought by popes in the end of 18th century and statues brought to Rome during the Roman Empire. Noteworthy are the precious sarcophagi dating from the 3rd and 2nd millennium B.C. and the statues that decorated the Villa of the Emperor Hadrian (117-138), exhibited in Room III, made of black basalt, imitating Egyptian statuary.

Golden mask of
a Sarcophagus

Statues from
Villa Adriana at Tivoli

Nile boat
wooden model

Chiaramonti Museum,
Dancing Maiden,
known as Gradiva

"Braccio Nuovo" Gallery,
Augustus of Prima Porta

Chiaramonti Museum

Founded by Pius VII Chiaramonti (1800-1823) for a collection of Roman busts and statues, the Museum was organized by the neo-classical sculptor Antonio Canova in 1807. There are about a thousand sculptures, including portraits of Emperors and gods, several fragments, friezes and relieves of sarcophagi. Noteworthy is a funerary monument of a miller dating from the 1st century A.D., which was found at Ostia.

Braccio Nuovo Gallery

Built by Pius VII and inaugurated in 1822.
It contains Roman statues and Roman copies of Greek original statues; mosaics are set on the floors.
The most remarkable works are the following: a statue of Augustus found at Prima Porta (north of Rome); a Roman copy of the Doryphorus from an original by the Greek sculptor Polykleitos (440 B.C.); two splendid gilded bronze peacocks, that may come from Hadrian's Mausoleum, copies of which are in the Courtyard of the "Pigna"; the statue of Nile, a Roman copy of a 1st century Hellenistic statue originally found in the Temple of Isis, near the Pantheon and showing the great Egyptian river with its tributaries.

Square Vestibule
with the statue of
Apoxyomenos
in the background

Pius-Clementine Museum

Commissioned by Popes Clement XIV (1769-1774) and Pius VI (1775-1799) to collect the most important Greek and Roman masterpieces in the Vatican.
After passing through a square vestibule and a small room with a magnificent marble cup, the visitor enters the Cabinet of Apoxyomenos, named after a Roman copy of an original Greek bronze work by Lysippos (c. 320 B.C.): it shows an athlete scrapping off his sweat with a strigil, a kind of razor used in antiquity; he gazes in the distance and his body is relaxing after the victory. Bramante's Staircase can be seen from the next room: it was commissioned by Julius II in 1512 as a link between the Palace of Innocent VIII (1484-1492) and the city of Rome: the spiral staircase, built in a square tower, could also be climbed on horseback.
The visitor can then reach the Octagonal Courtyard, named after its shape by Clement XIV in 1772. Among the most famous statues: the Belvedere Apollo, a Roman 2nd century copy from a Greek bronze original possibly by Leochares (330-320 B.C.), placed in the Agora of Athens: the statue of the God of Beauty, who probably carried a bow in his upraised arm and an arrow in his lowered hand, was considered an ideal of formal perfection and technical virtuosity in the Neo-classical period and was brought to the Vatican by Julius II; the celebrated Laocoon group, found in Rome on the Esquiline Hill in 1506, is a 1st century Roman copy from the Greek original in bronze by Hagesandros, Athanadoros and Polydoros. Soon much admired by Michelangelo, it was purchased by Julius II who had it set in the Vatican.
The sculpture represents the Trojan priest Laocoon who warned his fellow citizens about the ruse of the wooden horse, a gift of the Greeks, so he was condemned to die by the wrath of Athena with his two sons, victim of some serpents emerging from the sea; the

Cabinet of Apoxyomenos,
Apoxyomenos

Octagonal Courtyard,
Belvedere Apollo

Octagonal Courtyard,
Laocoon group

Room of the Muses,
Belvedere "Torso"

Perseus with the head of Medusa between two boxers by Antonio Canova (1800-1801).

Next to the courtyard are the following:

- Room of the Animals, with a collection of Roman statues and animals, heavily restored at the end of the 18th century.
- Gallery of Statues, originally open loggia of the Palace of Innocent VIII, later walled in during the second half of the 18th century. It contains precious Roman statues, including some copies of Greek statues of the Classical period (5th-4th century B.C.), such as the Apollo "Sauroktonos", the lizard-killer, copied from Praxiteles (c.350 B.C.) and the famous Sleeping Ariadne, a Roman copy of the 2nd century from an original by the School of Pergamon (2nd century B.C.).
- Room of Busts, mostly containing portraits of Roman emperors.
- Cabinet of Masks, with the remarkable Roman Venus of Cnidos; the original (mid 4th century B.C.) also by Praxiteles, came from the Greek sanctuary of Cnidos and was much admired in antiquity.
- Room of Muses, with Roman statues of muses and poets copied from Greek originals. The famous "Belvedere Torso", a 1st century B.C. original by the Athenian sculptor Apollonius, is in the middle of the room. The torso's powerful and vigorous musculature embodied Michelangelo's ideal and was much admired during the Renaissance and the neo-classical period. Recent studies identify the statue with the figure of the Greek hero Ajax who is meditating suicide.
- Round Room, built by Michelangelo Simonetti in the late

Gallery of Statues,
Sleeping Ariadne
in the background

18th century in a pure Neo-classical style. The dome is actually modelled on the Pantheon and has a diameter of 21.60 metres. A huge round monolithic porphyry basin stands in the middle of the room: it measures almost five metres across, comes from the Domus Aurea and was brought here in the late 18th century. A 2nd century Hercules in gilded bronze found near the Theatre of Pompey and a 3rd century mosaic from the Baths of Otricoli (region Umbria) are also fascinating.

- Greek-cross Room, with a 3rd century mosaic from Tusculum in

the middle and two colossal sarcophagi in red porphyry: the one on the left (4th century) belonged to Saint Helen, Constantine's mother (306-337), and comes from her mausoleum in Via Labicana; the sarcophagus on the right belonged to Costantina, Emperor Constantine's daughter and was in the Church of Saint Constance in Via Nomentana.
Going back to the Simonetti Staircase, the visitor may either visit the Etruscan Museum, housed in the Palace of Innocent VIII (1484-1492) or move on to Raphael's Rooms and the Sistine Chapel.

Etruscan Museum,
Room of the "Stones"

Etruscan Museum

Founded in 1837 by Pope Gregory XVI, the museum contains vases, bronzes and other archaeological findings from southern Etruria, a large collection of Hellenistic Italian vases and some Roman pieces (Antiquarium Romanorum). In Room II is the notable Regolini-Galassi tomb and Rooms IV-VIII, known as of the "Precious", exhibit gold jewellery realized by Etruscan goldsmiths during the ten centuries of their civilization.

Gallery of the Candelabra

Chariot Room

This late 18th century room contains a large marble Roman chariot drawn by two horses, dating from the 1st century A.D., but heavily restored in 1788. The copy of the famous Discobolus found in Villa Adriana at Tivoli, from a bronze Greek original by Myron (c. 460 B.C.) is also displayed here.

Gallery of the Candelabra

Originally an open loggia built in 1761, the loggia was walled up at the end of the 18th century.
The ceiling was painted in 1883-1887. The gallery contains Roman copies of Hellenistic originals (3rd–2nd century B.C.) and some great 2nd century candelabra, from Otricoli.

Gallery of Tapestries

Flemish tapestries, realized in Brussels by Pieter van Aelst's School from drawings by Raphael's pupils, during the pontificate of Clement VII (1523-1534), hang on the walls.
They were first shown in the Sistine Chapel in 1531, and arranged for the exhibition in this Gallery in 1838.

Gallery of Maps

It takes its name from the 40 maps frescoed on the walls, which represent the Italian regions and the papal properties at the time of Pope Gregory XIII (1572-1585). They were painted between 1580 and 1585 on drawings by Ignazio Danti, a famous geographer of the time.
Considering the Apennines as a partition element, on one side the regions surrounded by the Ligure and Tyrrhenian Seas are represented; on the other, the regions surrounded by the Adriatic Sea. The map of the main city accompanies each regional map.

Gallery of Maps, Etruria

Apartment of Pius V

This Apartment consists of a gallery, two small rooms and a chapel. It was built for Pope Pius V (1566-1572) and frescoed by Giorgio Vasari and Federico Zuccari. It contains Flemish tapestries of the 15th and 16th centuries. The first of the two small rooms, next to the gallery, contains a rich Mediaeval and Renaissance collection of ceramics found in the Vatican Palaces and in other Vatican properties in Rome; the other room has a suggestive collection of minute mosaics, made in Rome between the end of the 18th and the first half of the 19th century.

The Immaculate Conception and Sobieski Rooms

The Sobieski Room derives its name from the large painting by the Polish painter Jean Matejko (1838-1893), which represents Polish King John III Sobieski's victory over the Turks in Vienna in 1683. All the other paintings in the room date from the 19th century, as well as those in the Room of the Immaculate. The latter contains a big showcase, a gift from the French company Christofle, full of books given to Pius IX (1846-1878) by kings, bishops, cities and dioceses, when the dogma of the Immaculate Conception was established.

Raphael's Rooms

The "Vatican Rooms" were actually the apartments of Pope Julius II (1503-1513), who did not want to live in the rooms inhabited by his predecessor Alexander VI and frescoed by Pinturicchio, and, therefore, moved to the floor above into a wing built by Nicholas V in the 15th century. More famous artists such as Raphael's master, Perugino, had already worked on the rooms, but Pope Julius II gave Raphael (1483-1520) complete license and he erased all previous work.

Room of the Segnatura,
School of Athens

The rooms were painted in this chronological order: Room of the Segnatura in 1508-1511, Room of Heliodorus in 1511-1514, Room of the Fire in the Borgo in 1514-1517 and Room of Constantine in 1517-1524. This description will follow the compulsory route sequence.
The Room of Constantine was on the most part painted by Raphael's pupils after the master died suddenly on April 6th, 1520. Among the most important painters of the cycle, we quote Giulio Romano and Francesco Penni.

Room of the Segnatura, Disputation of the Most Holy Sacrament

The episodes depicted are: the "Baptism of Constantine", in the Basilica of St John Lateran, right of the entrance; the "Vision of the Cross" on the opposite wall; the "Battle at Milvio Bridge" on the wall opposite the windows showing Constantine with the cross that foretold his victory over the pagan Maxentius and finally, the "Donation of Constantine", set inside St Peter's, is on the window side of the room, showing the act which supposedly gave origin to the Church State (this actually occurred in 756, when Pippin, king of the Franks, gave the Holy See the lands of Central Italy).
The ceiling was painted by Tommaso Laureti in 1585 and shows the "Triumph of Christianity" over paganism, represented by the statue that has fallen and broken.
Next the visitor enters the most ancient part of the 2nd century Pontifical Palace; the Room of the Chiaroscuri was frescoed in the second decade of the 16th century using Raphael's drawings, while the Niccolina Chapel, private chapel of Nicholas V, was painted between 1447 and 1451 by Fra Angelico, a Dominican monk devoted to miniatures, who depicted here the Stories of Saint Stephen and Saint Lawrence.
Going back to the Rooms, there is the Room of Heliodorus, which was the first to be painted by Raphael, between 1511 and 1514.

Room of the Segnatura, Parnassus

Here its recurring theme of God assisting mankind glorifies the Church's spiritual and temporal power. The "Mass of Bolsena" represents a miracle, which supposedly occurred in 1263, when drops of blood fell from the Host, convincing a Bohemian priest about the transubstantiation (transformation) of the bread and wine into Christ's body and blood. Julius II, who commissioned the work, is shown taking part in the mass. The "Expulsion of Heliodorus" from the Temple of Jerusalem represents the sacredness of Church property: Heliodorus, after stealing the treasure in the Jewish Temple of Jerusalem, is captured by Gods' messengers, while a group of people including Julius II watch the scene. Compared to the "School of Athens", discussed later on, the empty central space of the painting and the dark colours are surely influenced by the Venetian painting of the period. The "Liberation of Saint Peter " is also painted in dark tones; in fact it is one of the first Italian night scenes in art history. The fresco has three scenes: the angel asking Saint Peter to follow him (centre), Saint Peter escaping and the angel (right), the guards waking up in a magnificent moonlight (left).
The first room painted by Raphael, the Room of the Segnatura, comes next. It derives its name from the function of the room, as it was the papal library where official acts were signed. The three Neoplatonic

Room
of the Fire in Borgo,
Fire in the Borgo

categories of Truth, Goodness and Beauty are represented here. The supernatural Truth is represented in the Disputation of the Most Holy Sacrament, rational Truth is in the School of Athens, Goodness is in the figures of Virtues and Law, while Beauty is represented in the Parnassus.

The "Disputation of the Most Holy Sacrament" shows below, two groups of ecclesiastics standing on either side of an altar with a monstrance, "discussing" the "truths" of heaven; above, on a cloud-borne semi-circle, sit saints and prophets, conversing peacefully, since they could see in Heaven what had already been promised on earth. Christ, with the Madonna and Saint John is above them, with the dove, symbol of the Holy Spirit, at his feet; God the father dominates the whole scene. The floor perspective has its vanishing point in the monstrance, the central point of the composition. The "School of Athens" is one of Raphael's most famous paintings: two figures, Plato and Aristotle, stand out against an ancient architectural background, probably symbolizing the new St Peter's. Plato resembles Leonardo

and points towards the sky, alluding to the world of ideas, while Aristotle turns down the palm of his hand, a reference to the rational principles of his philosophy. A multitude of philosophers surround these two great thinkers of the ancient world, each resembling men of Raphael's time. They include Heracleitus (Michelangelo), Euclid (Bramante) who is drawing a geometric figure on the blackboard, Diogenes, almost reclining on the steps, Ptolemy and Zoroaster respectively holding the globe and the celestial sphere in their hands. The second character on the right wearing a green cap is Raphael's self-portrait. Apollo, surrounded by muses, famous poets and men of letters, is represented in the "Parnassus". Homer, with his face turned upwards towards the sky, can be seen on the left and Dante is shown in profile.

The paintings in the last room were commissioned by Leo X Medici (1513-1521) and show famous historical events which occurred during the pontificates of those popes, named "Leo". The room is named after the main fresco, the "Fire in the Borgo", representing a miracle performed by Leo IV in 847, when the Pope extinguished a huge fire in the area around the Vatican basilica, simply by appearing at the benediction loggia and making the sign of the cross. The other frescoes realized by great Raphael's assistants, are: the "Oath of Leo III", the "Crowning of Charlemagne" by Pope Leo III in the year 800, and "The Battle of Ostia", showing Leo IV defeating the Saracens in 849 along the Roman coast.

Room
of the Fire in Borgo,
The Battle of Ostia

Raphael's Loggia

Construction on the "Loggias" began in 1508, under the architect Donato Bramante; after his death (1514), Raphael took over and also painted the frescoes on the second level.
Raphael's pupils assisted with the painting: these frescoes are a pictorial response to Raphael's rivalry with Michelangelo, since many of the themes taken from the Genesis and represented in the Sistine Chapel are also touched on in the Loggia.
16th century painters Giovanni da Udine, Giulio Romano and Perin del Vaga did the frescoes on the first and third floors.
The "grotesque" decorations are particularly noteworthy, with vegetable motifs and bizarre human figures and animals, inspired by paintings in the newly discovered residence of Emperor Nero (54-64), the Domus Aurea.

Borgia Apartment

This was a private wing built for Alexander VI (1492-1503) and decorated by Bernardo di Betto, called il Pinturicchio and his assistants. After the pontiff's death, the work on the apartments stopped. They were only re-opened to the public at the end of the 19th century. Most of the rooms are now used for the Collection of Modern Religious Art, inaugurated by Paul VI in 1973. This Collection hosts about 600 accumulated works of painting, sculpture and graphic, through donations of contemporary Italian and foreign artists and includes works by Gaugin, Chagall, Klee and Kandinskij.

Raphael's Loggia,
XI Bay

Sistine Chapel

The Sistine Chapel is named after his commissioner, Sixtus IV della Rovere (1471-1484), who decided to have a large room built where the "Cappella Magna" once stood. The "Cappella Magna" was a mediaeval fortified hall that the Papal Court used for assemblies. At that time, it was made up of about 200 members: a college of 20 cardinals, representatives of religious orders and important families, a choir, and a large number of laymen and servants. The Sistine construction was also to be a defensive structure, warding off both the Medici family, because of the continuous tension between the rulers of Florence and the Pope, and Muhammad II's Turks, who at that time were threatening the western coast of Italy. Its construction started in 1475, during the Jubilee Year proclaimed by Sixtus IV, and ended in 1483, when on August 15th the Pope solemnly inaugurated the new Chapel dedicated to Our Lady of the Assumption. The project, designed by Baccio Pontelli, included the use of a third of the height of the existing mediaeval walls.
According to some scholars, the dimensions of the hall (40.23 metres in length, 13.40 metres in width and 20.70 metres in height) are copied from Solomon's great temple in Jerusalem, which was destroyed by the Romans in 70 A.D.
The main entrance to the Chapel, located opposite the small entrance used today, is preceded by the imposing Sala Regia built for papal audiences. Arched windows light the chapel, while lunettes and triangular webs join the ceiling's barrel vault with the side walls. A choir once used the stalls on the right, while the Papal Court sat on the stone benches along three sides of the hall, excluding the altar side. An elegant 15th century balustrade surmounted by candelabra divides the area destined to the clergy from the area used by the public; at the end of the 16th century the balustrade was pushed back to make the former area larger. The splendid 15th century mosaic floor was copied from mediaeval models and is completely original.
After the architectural structure was completed in 1481, Sixtus IV summoned various Florentine painters to work in the chapel, including

Botticelli, Ghirlandaio, Cosimo Rosselli, Signorelli and Umbrian artists such as Perugino and Pinturicchio.
They were asked to paint the side walls, divided horizontally in three sections and vertically spaced by elegant pilasters. Damask-like draperies with the pope's coat of arms were frescoed on the lower part of the walls. Tapestries were hung above the draperies; some of them made by Raphael and his assistants in the second decade of the 16th century, can now be seen in the room dedicated to Raphael in the Vatican Pinacoteca. The middle section, the most important area, was painted with Biblical scenes from the lives of Moses and Christ, both seen as liberators of humanity. To stress the continuity between his pontificate and his predecessors', Sixtus IV had the upper section, at window-level, decorated with portraits of the early pontiffs from the 1st century to the beginning of the 4th century, each in a monochromatic niche.
Finally, golden stars on a blue background were painted on the chapel ceiling by Pier Matteo d'Amelia, as can be seen in a famous 16th century drawing now in the Uffizi. The chapel's decoration was completed by Sixtus IV's nephew, Giuliano della Rovere, who became Pope Julius II (1503-1513). He planned to renew the whole city of Rome, and to realize this grandiose task he summoned Michelangelo Buonarroti (1475-1564), who was already well known in Florence and had previously worked for the new pope. After some initial contention, Michelangelo agreed to fresco the vault. It took four years of hard work to complete the painting (from 1508 to 1512), and Michelangelo's theme was the history of mankind before the coming of Christ.
Later on, between 1536 and 1541, Michelangelo also painted the "Last Judgement", commissioned by Paul III Farnese (1534-1549), who confirmed the commission made by his predecessor, Clement VII (1523-1534). The theme represented is mankind's inevitable Fate and God as the absolute judge of man's destiny.

- **Biblical stories on the side walls**

Painted on the walls are the following: on the left, looking at the "Last Judgement", scenes from the Old Testament, with the Stories of Moses, saviour of the Jewish people; on the right, scenes from the New Testament, with the Stories of Christ, the saviour of all humanity. These scenes are therefore parallel. Originally this wall also included the "Finding of Moses" and the "Nativity of Jesus", but Michelangelo later obliterated them in 1534. This cycle ends on the main entrance wall with "Disputation over the Body of Moses" and the "Resurrection of Christ", both re-painted in the 16th century. The captions above, restored recently, are "tituli" referring to the paintings below.

Left Wall,
Perugino,
The Journey of Moses in Egypt

Left Wall,
Botticelli,
Trials of Moses

- The left wall
The first painting, "The Journey of Moses in Egypt", attributed to Perugino, represents a scene when "Moses (...) took his wife and sons and, putting them on a donkey, started back for Egypt; and Moses took the staff of God in his hand" (Exodus 4:20). During the Journey, an angel stops Moses - and here the painting differs from the original story - who orders him to circumcise his second son (on the right). Next is the "Trials of Moses", painted by Botticelli and his assistants. This is one of the most complex paintings, since there are so many different episodes represented. One can see (from the right): the killing of an Egyptian who had hit a Jew, the flight into Madian, local maidens meeting and watering their herds, the Lord appearing from a burning bush (left) and above, in the centre, God appearing to Moses, asking him to take his shoes off in His presence (Exodus 2:11-20 and 3:1-6). The two superb female figures in the foreground are typical of Botticelli. The "Passage of the Red Sea" is attributed to the Florentine painter Biagio d'Antonio (1446-1516). Moses and his people, fleeing from Egypt and the Pharaoh's army, cross the Red Sea when God parts the waters for them; then the sea closes, killing the pressing Egyptians (Exodus 14:23-30). In the lower left, a woman plays a hymn of thanks to the Lord (Exodus 15:1-20).
The "Handing Over of the Tables of the Law", attributed to Cosimo Rosselli and Piero di Cosimo, illustrates the Bible's account of the Golden Calf. Moses had climbed Mount Sinai to receive the tables of the Law (Exodus 23:12-15) and after they had waited for him, the Jews gathered around the priest Aaron. Then, gathering rings and other gold objects, they forged a golden calf, placed it on an altar and began to worship it. When Moses came back from the mountain with the tables and saw that his people had disobeyed the prohibition to make sacred images, he broke the tables in fury (Exodus 32:1-19). Botticelli's "Punishment of Korah, Dathan and Abiram" refers to when the Jews revolted against the Lord during their Journey to the Promised Land. They complained about the terrible conditions in which Moses forced them to live, but God punished them: suddenly the earth parted under their feet, swallowing them and all their possessions (Numbers, 16). The Arch of Constantine can be seen in the background of this scene.
The "Legacy and Death of Moses " by Signorelli also includes several different episodes: on the right, Moses blesses the Israelites (Deuteronomy, 33) and on the left, he gives the holy rod to Joshua. An angel in the upper centre points toward the promised land, and the death of Moses is shown on the left.
- The right wall
The "Baptism of Christ", with episodes taken from the Gospel of Matthew, is by Perugino. John preaching before the Baptism of Christ appears on the left; the baptism scene is in the foreground and Jesus preaching to his followers is on the right. The Holy Trinity can be seen

Right Wall,
Ghirlandaio,
Calling of the first apostles

in the middle of the fresco, with the dove of the Holy Spirit, enclosed in a circle, hovering above Christ and the Eternal Father surrounded by angels.
The second panel contains the "Temptations of Christ" and "Cleansing of the Leper" by Botticelli, also taken from Matthew's Gospel. Satan's vain attempts to corrupt Christ and induce him to worship Satan are portrayed here (challenging him to turn stones into bread, to throw himself from a temple and be saved by angels, and offering him the world's beauties, seen from a precipice; Matthew 4:1-11). The leper in the centre is purified according to a Jewish ritual. In the background,

Right Wall,
Cosimo Rosselli,
Sermon on the mount

the façade of the hospital of Saint Spirit can be seen; built by Pope Sixtus IV, the hospital is located between Via della Conciliazione and the Tiber.
The "Calling of the first Apostles" by Ghirlandaio is a faithful rendering of the Gospel text (Matthew 4:18-22), which shows Jesus asking Peter and Andrew (on the left), two brothers who were fishermen, to kneel in front of Him (foreground) and calling out to Jacob and John, in a boat, to come to him (upper right).
The "Sermon on the Mount" (Matthew 5:1-12) is attributed to Cosimo Rosselli and shows Christ curing the leper (Matthew 8:1-4) on the right, Christ pronouncing the famous Beatitudes, on the left. This painting is correlated to the opposite painting where Moses receives the Tables of the Law.
The "Handing over of the Keys " of the Church from Jesus to St Peter is by Perugino and it is probably the most beautiful painting on the Sistine Chapel's walls.
A typical Renaissance octagonal temple stands in the background of the floor in perspective, with two triumphant arches beside it resembling the Arch of Constantine in Rome, which allude to continuity between past and present.
Cosimo Rosselli and Biagio d'Antonio's "Last Supper" has a distinctive, semi-octagonal table and its shape is echoed by the walls and ceiling. Judas has his back to the viewer and a small devil on his shoulder. Scenes of Christ praying in the garden, his arrest and the Crucifixion are in the background.

The Ceiling

This is Michelangelo's masterpiece and one of the most important painting cycles in the world, covering 800 sq metres of wall with "good fresco" painting.
It was begun in May 1508, and then stopped for about a year between September 1510 and August 1511. The chapel was solemnly inaugurated by Julius II on November 1st, 1512.
The vault's iconography is linked to the themes chosen for the side walls, representing humanity's long wait for Christ, the prophecies foreseeing his coming and scenes from the Genesis. All the figures are set in a massive, architectural painted background, which is superimposed to the real vault.
Interpretation of the paintings can be divided into three parts:
The first part: Christ's Ancestors according to Matthew's Gospel (1:1-17) are in the triangular webs and lunettes above the Windows. Men and women, representing humanity in general and generations succeeding one another, are crowded into a narrow, shallow space, awaiting the great event of Revelation in different poses and attitudes: they look tired, exhausted, in fact, prostrated and often in great pain caused by their inactivity, exasperated by the interminably slow passage of time before the birth of Christ.
The painter's extraordinary technical ability is particularly noticeable

Michelangelo,
Creation of Adam,
detail

ERITHRAEA
EZECHIEL

DANIEL
PERSICHA

in some of the figures, such as Mathan (above the original entrance) or Josaphat (in the central part of the vault, near the episodes from the life of Christ), rapidly frescoed with quick brush strokes and very fluid colours.
The four pendentives are painted with scenes alluding to the Salvation of Israel's people. Beginning from the part over the ancient entrance are the following:

- on the right, "Judith and Holofernes". The Babylonian king Nabucodonosor had ordered his Assyrian general Holofernes to attack the Israeli army; Judith, a young Jewish girl, got Holofernes drunk and then killed him. The scene shows Judith giving his head to her maid (Judith 13:8-10).
- on the left, the episode with "David and Goliath". During the war between the Jews and the Philistines, young David fought Goliath, a

Michelangelo,
Creation of the
Celestial Bodies
and Plants

Michelangelo,
Original Sin and
Expulsion from Paradise

giant who had sworn that he would reduce the Jews to slavery if he defeated their army (1, Samuel 17: 41-51).
The pendentives towards the *Last Judgement* wall represent:
- on the right, the "Brazen Serpent", alluding to the Biblical episode in which the Lord sent the reptiles against the Israelites. During their journey to the Promised Land, they became discouraged with the hardships endured, incurring the wrath of both God and Moses (Numbers 21:8). They repented for their behaviour, however, and

Michelangelo,
The Flood

were pardoned. God then told Moses to make a serpent in bronze: looking at this bronze serpent could save anyone bitten by one of the reptiles;
- on the left, the "Punishment of Haman", an episode from the Book of Esther. A young vizier named Haman issued an edict against the Jews, ordering that anyone refusing to bow down to the king would be killed. Esther, the wife of a Persian king, managed to have the edict annulled, thereby saving the people of Israel and causing the death of the vizier Haman.

Michelangelo,
Prophet Isaiah

Michelangelo,
Prophet Daniel

Michelangelo,
Prophet Joel

Above these pendentives are symmetrical bronze nudes and "bucrani" (ox skulls), classical decorative motifs alluding to sacrificial rituals.
The second part: splendid figures of the seven Prophets of the Bible and of the five pagan Sibyls, seated on massive thrones, outlined by naked, monochrome naked puttos resting on plinths. The Prophets and Sibyls both predicted the coming of Christ. Each figure is accompanied by angels or puttos who underline the personage's specific role.
They are all caught in the act of reading a book or unrolling a parchment scroll, absorbed in an extraordinary physical and spiritual effort. The most beautiful figures are probably the Delphic Sibyl and the prophets Ezekiel and Jonah. Jonah is shown next to the whale inside which he remained for three days - the same amount of time that Christ stayed in the sepulchre before his Resurrection.
The third part: the rectangles in the middle have nine scenes from the Genesis, four of them large ones and five small ones. Three of these episodes describe the Creation, three the story of Adam, and three deal with Noah. Michelangelo started painting the vault with the Noah episodes, probably intending to paint the scenes with the Creator at a later moment.
The three scenes of the Creation start with the "Separation of Light from Darkness"(Genesis 1:3-4), showing God wrapped in pink drapery and occupying most of the scene, which has an extremely complex perspective. Recent studies done after the fresco was cleaned have proved that Michelangelo painted it in just one day.
Next is the extraordinary "Creation of Celestial Bodies and Plants", divided into two asymmetric parts, each one containing the figure of the Lord. On the right He faces outwards, creating the shining sun and the pale moon with one sweeping gesture, while on the left the Lord has his back to the viewer as He creates plant life (Genesis 1:12-16).
The third panel, with the "Separation of Land from Sea" (Genesis 1: 7-9), shows a completely new perspective and is equally beautiful.
Next to it is the celebrated "Creation of Adam", where the focal point, the two loosened hands of the protagonists, is slightly off-centre. Adam's body is magnificent. God is wrapped in pink drapery, and wingless angels with an expression of amazement on their faces, support His impetus. It is interesting to note that the two figures of God and Adam were actually painted using a single preliminary cartoon, as if Michelangelo were confirming what is written in the Bible: "God created man in the image of himself" (Genesis 1:27).

I O E L

The "Creation of Eve" is next. It should be noted that in Michelangelo's fresco Eve is born from living rock and not, as the Bible says, from Adam's rib.
The sixth panel is occupied by the "Original Sin" (left) and the "Expulsion from Paradise" (right). The two scenes are divided by the tree of good and evil, with the serpent coiled around its trunk and the Archangel Gabriel above it. The tree is slightly off-centre, marking the transition from lush countryside to an arid landscape, expressing how the human condition has changed. Even our ancestors' bodies change after the Sin, seeming to age, which proves that physical appearance for Michelangelo also represents inner spirituality.
The seventh episode, "Sacrifice of Noah", shows the Patriarch thanking the Lord after the flood. The offering of a ram's entrails can be seen in the foreground: "Then Noah built an altar to the Lord and, taking some of all the clean animals and clean birds, he sacrificed burnt offerings on it" (Genesis 8:20).
The "Flood" in the eighth panel is largely taken from the seventh and eighth chapters of the Genesis. A tent, where the terrified future victims of the flood are taking shelter, is on the right. In the centre, Noah carries the few survivors to safety on a boat, taking them towards the arc in the upper left of the painting, which symbolises the Church. The scene of Salvation is painted diagonally in the foreground: after the inundation, the waters have retreated and the survivors can settle down on dry land, along with the few possessions they have saved. Sixty people crowd into this scene, standing out against a light background in a deep landscape.
This was probably the first episode painted by Michelangelo: afterwards he preferred larger images, daringly foreshortened and the composition became complex. Unfortunately, part of the sky collapsed in 1797 when Castel Sant'Angelo's gunpowder depot exploded; 16th century prints show that a thunderbolt was painted in the collapsed area.
In the ninth panel over the original entrance to the Chapel is the "Drunkenness of Noah" (Genesis 9:20-23), showing life and agricultural activities resuming on earth. " Noah, a man of the soil, proceeded to plant a vineyard. When he drank some of its wine, he became drunk and lay uncovered inside his tent. Ham, the father of Canaan, saw his father's nakedness and told that to his two brothers outside. But Shem and Japheth took a garment and laid it across their shoulders; then they walked in backward and covered their

EZECHIEL

Michelangelo,
Libyan Sibyl

Michelangelo,
Delphic Sibyl

Michelangelo,
Prophet Jeremiah

father's nakedness. Their faces were turned the other way so that they would not see their father's nakedness".
The Genesis scenes are surrounded by "Ignudi", extraordinary naked male figures; their powerful bodies probably represent male beauty, created in God's image.
They sit on marble blocks in "spiralling" poses, holding festoons or ribbons with large bronze medallions painted with scenes from the Old Testament. Their role in the composition is an important one, because they break up the structure's regularity, visually connecting the Genesis panels. It has been observed that "their presence on each of the four relieves very naturally frames the smaller scenes, and their function in the sequence of the nine panels is therefore essential" (R. Pane, 1964). This function is particularly noticeable between the first and second scene, where part of the fresco over the arch collapsed in 1797.
Other important painting effects are the following: the way the painter enlarged the naked male figures and the figure of Christ towards the altar; his diversified use of colour, which is applied thickly in the Moses scenes and with rapid brush strokes in the last scenes.
Finally, the images in the foreground have clear, sharp outlines, while those in the background have softened outlines painted with fluid brush strokes, a technique which Michelangelo had probably learnt from his contemporary, Leonardo.

Michelangelo,
Cumaen Sibyl

The Last Judgement

In 1532, twenty years after Michelangelo finished the ceiling, Clement VII (1523-1534) asked him to paint the far wall of the Sistine Chapel. Work began only under the next pope, Paul III Farnese (1534-1549), and the magnificent fresco was finally unveiled during an official ceremony on October 13th, 1541.
The painting also symbolised the Papacy's regained supremacy, after the tragic events of 1527, when the Lansquenets, German mercenary troops, sacked Rome, and the Lutheran crisis which had undermined the Roman Church's authority.
First of all, Michelangelo lined the wall to be painted with a layer of brick. To prevent dust from settling on it and improve the perspective, this new surface was angled slightly outwards at the top (26 cm). Some 15th century frescoes were thereby lost and so were the lunettes Michelangelo painted.
Although Michelangelo was inspired by the Bible, particularly by the Revelation, and by Dante's Divine Comedy, his own tragic

Michelangelo,
The Last Judgement,
detail,
Christ the Judge

IONAS

Michelangelo,
The Last Judgement,
detail,
Charon the Demon
leads the souls to Hell

Michelangelo,
The Last Judgement,
detail,
Angels with long Trumpets

Michelangelo,
The Last Judgement,
detail,
The Saved

philosophic vision prevails in this work. Christ, in the middle of the fresco with the Madonna beside him, decides the inevitable afterlife destiny of each human being with a simple gesture of his arms: some are saved (the figures on the left, rising to Heaven), but most are damned (the naked people on the right, plunging into Hell).
The figures move in a kind of vortex, against the background of a blue sky without any architectural structures. The dead, seen on the lower left, are woken from their long slumber by angels' trumpets, and their skeletons gradually transform back to being bodies.
These angels in the middle of the painting have no wings and hold up two books: the smaller book held by the Archangel Michael records the names of the blessed, while the larger book is a list of the damned. On Christ's left are Saint Andrew, seen from the back with his cross and Saint John the Baptist with a powerful physique, who might represent Adam.
Lower down are Saint Lawrence with a ladder, symbolising his martyrdom on a grate over hot coals and Saint Bartholomew, holding a fleshless human skin (some consider it a portrait of Michelangelo).
On the right are Saint Peter, actually a portrait of the commissioner pope, Paul III, holding a silver and a gold key; below Peter is Saint Blaise, with the iron combs used to torture him and Saint Catherine of Alexandria with the toothed crescent-knife of her martyrdom.
These two figures, particularly Saint Blaise, were heavily repainted in 1565 because they were thought indecent. Saint Sebastian kneels beside them, with arrows in his hand. Slightly below this, on the right, is the famous figure of a damned man who, frightened by the terrible sight, covers one eye. In another significant scene, the mythical boatman Charon, who ferried the damned in Virgil's Aeneid and Dante's Divine Comedy, actually pushes sinners out of his boat towards Hell, abandoning them to their dramatic fate. Biagio da Cesena, a well-known papal master of ceremonies at that time, is at the end of this group. He criticised Michelangelo's work, saying that it was worthy of a bath or tavern, and Michelangelo took revenge by using Biagio to represent Minos, one of the Underworld judges in Greek-Roman mythology, wrapped in serpents' coils that indicate to what circle of Hell the damned are destined.

Michelangelo,
The Last Judgement,
detail,
Saint Catherine
and Saint Blaise

Michelangelo,
The Last Judgement,
detail,
Resurrection of the Dead

At the very top of the fresco the symbols of Christ's passion can be seen: the cross, the crown of thorns, the dice used by the guards, the Flagellation column and the sponge with which he was wet. Here Michelangelo's style is quite different from that in the ceiling, and expresses his changed attitude towards life: God is the severe judge whom none can question, not even the Virgin Mary, and certainly not man.
This is why the bodies seem heavy with grief, as if they carried traces of their experiences on earth, which weighed them down. The colours stand out against an intense and dominating blue, generally changing from a whole gamut of reds to green, brown and black tones, which stress a tragic way of interpreting events. Only the background behind Christ and Mary, who has a light blue cape, is enlivened by an intense yellow that emphasizes the power of Christ's raised arm. The Council of Trent, ended in 1563, decreed that art works in sacred places had to be modest and completely respect the Scriptures. Because of this, the "Last Judgement" frescoes were somewhat repainted in 1565 by one of Michelangelo's pupils, Daniele da Volterra, who covered the figures' nakedness with famous veils and loincloths, earning the nickname of "il Braghettone" (the maker of breeches). Other repainting was done for the same reason in the late 16th century and during the next two centuries.
When the painting was restored, scholars debated intensely whether or not to remove these "dry" additions to the fresco, and argued on the one hand that Michelangelo's original work should be brought to light, and on the other that the additions were part of the frescos' life-story. Finally, they decided to keep only Daniele da Volterra's additions as the tangible expression of a historical era, and to remove all subsequent additions. This was because, as John Paul II said during the mass held when the Chapel was re-opened after restoration on April 8th 1994, "the Sistine Chapel is really the temple of the human body's divinity" and, "it bears witness to mankind's beauty as created by God, male and female"; in this beauty, Christ expressed "the whole mystery of the visibility of the invisible."

Michelangelo,
The Last Judgement,
detail,
Saint Bartholomew shows
the skin of the martyrdom

Michelangelo's painting technique and the Sistine Chapel restoration

The Sistine Chapel's accurate restoration was done between 1980 and 1994 by a group of experts from the Vatican Museums, co-ordinated by Director Carlo Pietrangeli. Professor Fabrizio Mancinelli, art historian, supervised the work and Gianluigi Colalucci was chief-restorer. The Ceiling frescoes were cleaned between 1980 and 1992, while the "Last Judgement" took four years of intense work, ending in 1994.
A new, completely forgotten Michelangelo emerged from the restoration. The candle smoke and even previous restorations (which consisted in painting over the frescos or retouching the colours to "brighten" them, which however deteriorated with the passing of time, thus making the frescoes even duller) had blackened the surface, so that in the past Michelangelo was commonly thought to be more interested in figures than in colour. After the cleaning, much art criticism on the artist had to be revised, or even completely re-written. The "re-discovered" colours are actually light, vivid and bright, very skilfully blended to reduce the flattening effect inevitably produced on the figures by distance.
The use of "bright colours" is particularly interesting. This means using a combination of strongly contrasting colours (such as in the Delphic Sibyl, the Prophet Daniel, or even more obviously in the pendentives and lunettes) to increase volume and emphasize the impact of the masses. Michelangelo used very thin, transparent colours on the Ceiling, sometimes applying them with quick, sure brush strokes that leave the background visible.
The figures in the foreground generally have sharp outlines, while those in the background are shaded and more sketchily coloured in, achieving the effect of a lens focusing on the nearest objects.
Michelangelo used only very high quality pigments for the colours and because of this the frescoes have lasted in time: ochre (earthy varieties of ore) provided the reds and yellows, iron silicates were used for the greens and lapis lazuli powder for the blues. The lilac is "morellone" (produced by a plant with purple flowers), and Michelangelo used what is commonly known as "Saint John's white" and charcoal for black. This restoration attracted worldwide interest. After some extremely careful lab tests, the first phase of restoration consisted in washing the frescoes with distilled water; then a mild solvent was applied to remove the layers of dirt, maintaining the frescoes' thin protective coating made up of a layer dust which deposited itself on them right after they were painted.
The Sistine Chapel is now climate controlled with air-conditioners and a sophisticated monitoring system verifies and checks the environmental conditions in the Chapel.

The Last Judgement, detail of Christ the Judge during the cleaning (1991)

Museums of the
Vatican Apostolic Library,
Sistine Hall

Vatican Apostolic Library

Founded by Popes Nicholas V (1451) and Sixtus IV (1475), the library was constantly enlarged. In 1589 Sixtus V built the wing across the Courtyard of "Belvedere", which contains the Sistine Hall, a grand reading room, named after the Pontiff and built by Domenico Fontana. Scholars must present a letter of recommendation to consult the library, which has about 50,000 manuscripts, 7,000 incunabula (books printed in the 15th century), engravings and about one million volumes.

ropa del sec. XVI

Library of the Pope

Pio-Christian Museum

Pio-Christian Museum, Good Shepherd

It contains Christian antiquities originally exhibited in the Lateran Museum. Founded by Pius IX in 1854, it consists of statues, sarcophagi, inscriptions and archaeological findings dating from the 6th century. Noteworthy is the statue of the Good Shepherd: it represents a beardless young man wearing a sleeveless tunic and a bag. The statue was restored in the 18th c.

Gregorian Profane Museum

Gregorian Profane Museum, group of Athena and Marsyas

The museum was founded by Gregory XVI (1831-1846) in the Lateran Palace in 1884 and John XXIII had it relocated in the Vatican in 1970. It contains Greek original works, Roman copies and sculptures dating from the 1st to the 3rd c. A.D. The most famous group is Athena and Marsyas, a copy of a Greek original by Myron (c. 450 B.C.).

Missionary Ethnological Museum, Plumed Serpent

Missionary Ethnological Museum

Inaugurated by Pius XI in 1926, this museum was also moved from the Lateran Palace. The collection consists of artworks and historical vestiges from missions all over the world. There are some interesting models of non-Catholic places of worship, such as Beijing's Temple of the Sky (originally from the 15th century but re-done in the 18th century), the Altar of Confucius and the Shintoist Temple of Nara, Japan's ancient capital city. The Buddhist devotional statues are testimonies of spiritual life in Tibet, Indonesia, India and the Far East; the findings of Islamic and Central African culture are also interesting, and so are objects and works of art, especially from Mexico, Guatemala and Nicaragua.

Historical Museum - The Carriage Pavilion

This museum was founded by Paul VI in 1973 and is located in a large room under the Square Garden.
It contains saddles, carriages, automobiles and sedan chairs used by various popes.
Curiosities include some 19th century carriages, a model of Vatican City's first train engine (1929) and a Berlin built for Leo XII, used by popes for gala occasions until Pius XI's time.
The Carriage Pavilion is a section of the Historical Museum and since 1991 it has been in the Papal Apartment of the Lateran Apostolic Palace.

The Carriage Pavilion, Citroën Lictoria

The Carriage Pavilion,
Great Gala Berlin

Vatican Gardens

These are pleasant to visit either on foot or by bus and are open to guided tour groups only. All the structures needed to make this small State work are inside the gardens, including the Palace of the Governorate, the Courthouse, the Train station, the main offices of Radio Vatican, a small heliport, the Pontifical Academy of Sciences and the Nervi Hall, built between 1966 and 1971 also for papal audiences. The Hall has 6,000 seats and standing room far another 4,000 people. Also found in the gardens is the artistically valuable "Casina" of Pius IV (1559-1565) built by architect Pirro Ligorio, with two buildings connected by an oval-shaped terrace.

Fountain of the "Galley"

Casina of Pius IV

LEO XII. PONTIFEX. MAXIMVS. FRONTEM. HANC. RENOVAVIT. PONT. AN. I.

Map of the Vatican City

1. Bronze Doors
2. Arch of the Bells
3. Petriano Entrance
4. Bastion of Nicholas V
5. Palace of Sixtus V
6. Palace of Gregory XIII
7. Mediaeval Palace
8. Borgia Tower
9. Sistine Chapel
10. Hall of Ligorio
11. Vatican Apostolic Library
12. Courtyard of the Library
13. "Braccio Nuovo" Gallery
14. Tower of the Winds
15. Hall of Bramante
16. Courtyard of the "Pigna"
17. Fountain of the "Galley"
18. Staircase of Bramante
19. Palace of Belvedere
20. Pius-Clementine Museum
21. Atrium of the Four Gates
22. Entrance to the Vatican Museums
23. Vatican Pinacoteca
24. Gregorian-Profane, Pio-Christian and Missionary Ethnological Museums
25. Museum of the Carriages
26. The "Passetto"
27. Saint Anne Entrance
28. Church of Saint Anne of the Palafrenieri
29. Courtyard of the Swiss Guards
30. Vatican Typography
31. Restoration Workshop of Tapestries
32. Church of Saint Pellegrino
33. L' Osservatore Romano
34. Central Post Office
35. Vatican Chemistry
36. Square of the Furnace
37. Fountain of the Most Holy Sacrament
38. "Casina" of Pius IV
39. Pontifical Academy of Sciences
40. House of the Gardener
41. Fountain of the "Aquilone"
42. Tower of the "Gallinaro"
43. Technical Management of Radio Vatican
44. Border of the Leonine City
45. Grotto of Lourdes
46. St John's Tower
47. Transmission Center "Marconi"
48. Ethiopian College
49. Building of the Governorate
50. Railway Station
51. Mosaic School
52. Church of Saint Stephen of the Abyssinians
53. Palace of the Tribunal
54. Residence of the Archpriest
55. Palace of Saint Charles
56. Saint Marta's Square
57. Domus Sanctae Marthae
58. Palace of the Canonicate and Sacristy of St Peter's
59. Square of the Roman Proto-martyrs
60. Teutonic College
61. Hall of the Papal Audiences
62. Palace of the Holy Office
63. Church of Saint Salvatore in Terrione

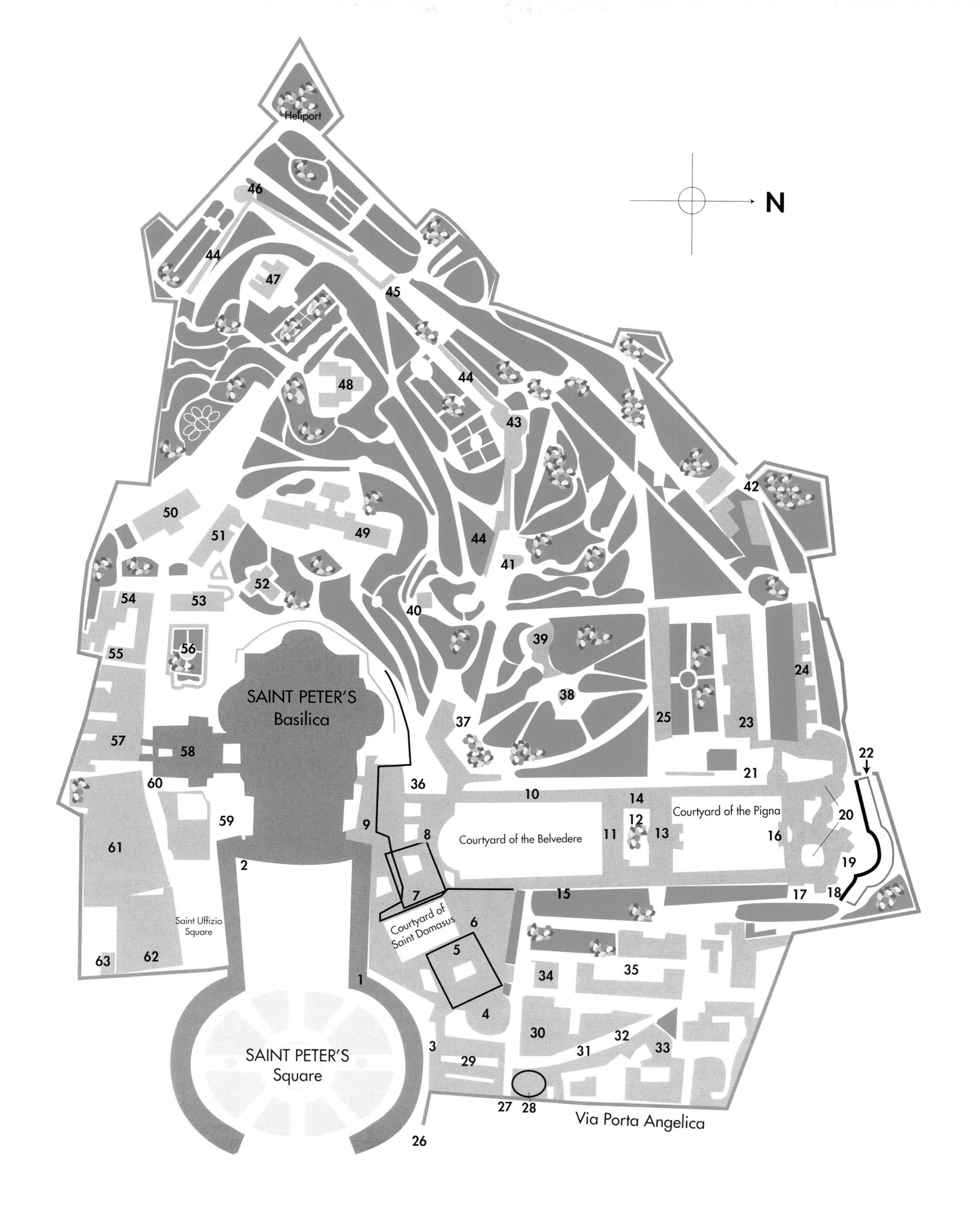
Heliport
N
SAINT PETER'S Basilica
Courtyard of the Belvedere
Courtyard of the Pigna
Courtyard of Saint Damasus
Saint Uffizio Square
SAINT PETER'S Square
Via Porta Angelica
1 2 3 4 5 6 7 8 9 10 11 12 13 14 15 16 17 18 19 20 21 22 23 24 25 26 27 28 29 30 31 32 33 34 35 36 37 38 39 40 41 42 43 44 45 46 47 48 49 50 51 52 53 54 55 56 57 58 59 60 61 62 63

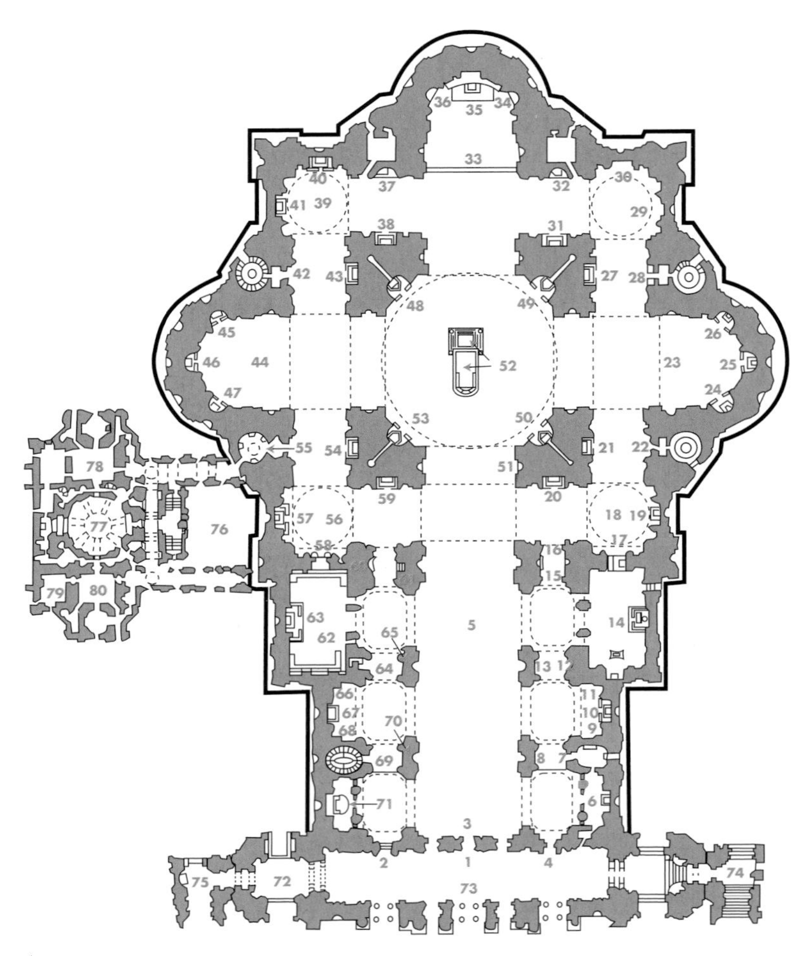

Map of Saint Peter's Basilica

LEGENDA

1 Atrium
2 Door of the Dead, by Manzù
3 Main Door, by Filarete
4 Holy Door
5 Nave
6 Chapel of the Pietà
7 Monument to Leo XII
8 Monument to Christine of Sweden
9 Monument to Pius XI
10 Chapel of St Sebastian
11 Monument to Pius XII
12 Monument to Innocent XII
13 Monument to the Countess Mathilda
14 Chapel of the Most Holy Sacrament
15 Monument to Gregory XIII
16 Monument to Gregory XIV
17 Monument to Gregory XVI
18 Gregorian Chapel
19 Altar of the Madonna del Soccorso
20 Altar of St Jerome
21 Altar of St Basil
22 Monument to Benedict XIV
23 Right transept
24 Altar of St Wenceslas
25 Altar of Sts Processo and Martiniano
26 Altar of St Erasmus
27 Altar of the Navicella
28 Monument to Clement XIII
29 Altar of St Michael Archangel
30 Altar of St Petronilla
31 Altar of St Peter with Tabitha
32 Monument to Clement X
33 Nave of the Cathedra
34 Monument to Urban VIII
35 St Peter's Cathedra
36 Monument to Paul III
37 Monument to Alexander VIII
38 Altar of St Peter healing the paralytic
39 Chapel of the Madonna of the Column
40 Altar of St Leo the Great
41 Altar of the Madonna of the Column
42 Monument to Alexander VII
43 Altar of the Sacred Heart
44 Left transept
45 Altar of St Thomas
46 Altar of St Joseph
47 Altar of St Peter's Crucifixion
48 Statue of St Veronica
49 Statue of St Helen
50 Statue of St Longinus
51 Statue of St Peter
52 Confession and Papal Altar
53 Statue of St Andrew
54 Altar of the "Bugia"
55 Monument to Pius VIII, Entrance to the Sacristy and Treasury
56 Clementine Chapel
57 Altar of St Gregory
58 Monument to Pius VII
59 Altar of the Transfiguration
60 Monument to Leo XI
61 Monument to Innocent XI
62 Chapel of the Choir
63 Chapel of the Immaculate Virgin Mary
64 Monument to St Pius X
65 Monument to Innocent VIII
66 Monument to John XXIII
67 Chapel of the Presentation of the Blessed Virgin
68 Monument to Benedict XV
69 Monument to M. Clementina Sobieski
70 Monument to the Stuarts
71 Baptistery
72 Arch of Bells
73 Mosaic of the "Navicella"
74 Equestrian statue of Constantine
75 Equestrian statue of Charlemagne
76 Largo Braschi
77 Sacristy
78 Historical Artistic Museum St Peter's Treasury
79 Chapter
80 Canons' Sacristy

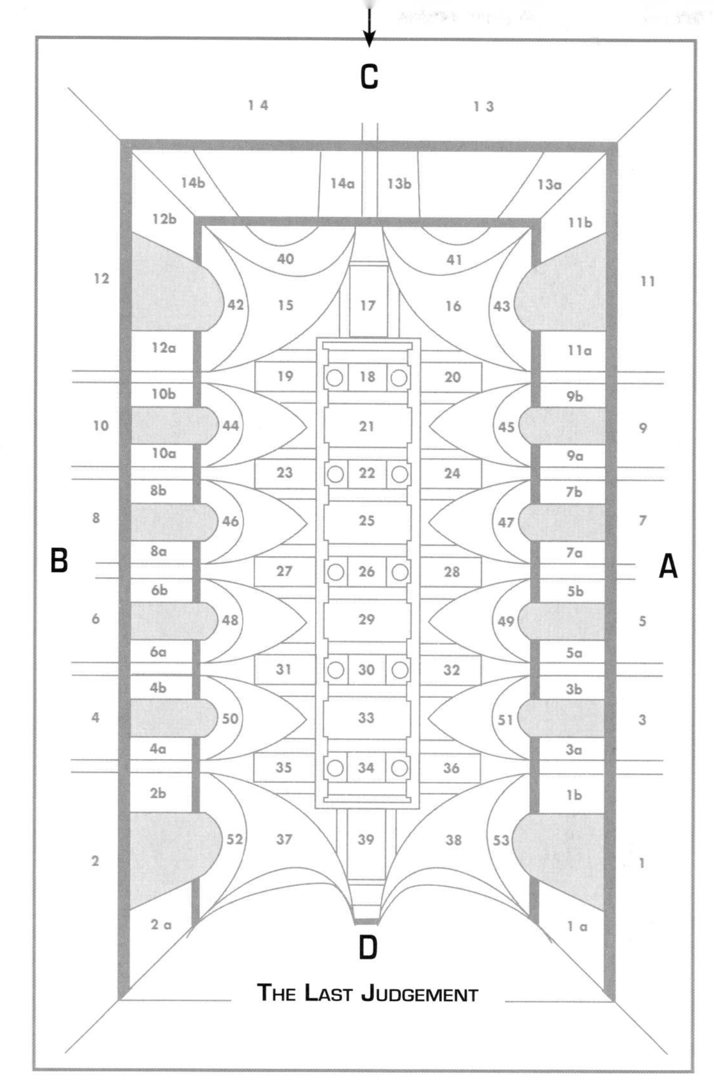

LEGENDA
A Wall with **Stories of Moses**
B Wall with **Stories of Christ**
C Entrance **Wall**
D Wall with the **Last Judgement**

Map of the Sistine Chapel

Wall A

1 **The Journey of Moses in Egypt**, Perugino
1A Pope Clement I
1B Pope Evaristus
3 **Trials of Moses**, Botticelli
3A Pope Sixtus I
3B Pope Iginus
5 **Passage of the Red Sea**, Biagio d'Antonio
5A Pope Anicetus
5B Pope Eleutherus
7 **Handing over of the Tables of the Law**, C. Rosselli
7A Pope Zephirinus
7B Pope Urban I
9 **Punishment of Korah, Dathan e Abiram**, Botticelli
9A Pope Anterus, Fra Diamante
9B Pope Cornelius
11 **Legacy and Death of Moses**, Luca Signorelli
11A Pope Stephen I
11B Pope Dionysius

Entrance wall, side A

13 **Disputation over the Body of Moses**, Matteo da Lecce
13A Pope Eutychianus, Ghirlandaio
13B Pope Marcellus I

Wall B

2 **Baptism of Christ**, Perugino
2A Pope Anacletus
2B Pope Alexander I
4 **Temptations of Christ**, Botticelli
4A Pope Telesphorus
4B Pope Pius I
6 **Calling of the first Apostles**, Ghirlandaio
6A Pope Soter
6B Pope Victor
8 **Sermon on the Mount**, C. Rosselli
8A Pope Callistus I
8B Pope Pontianus
10 **Handing over the Keys**, Perugino
10A Pope Fabian
10B Pope Lucius I
12 **Last Supper**, C. Rosselli, B. d'Antonio
12A Pope Sixtus II, Botticelli
12B Pope Felix I

Entrance wall, side B

14 **Resurrection of Christ**, H. van den Broeck
14A Pope Marcellinus
14B Pope Caius

Ceiling

15 Pendentive Judith and Holofernes
16 Pendentive David and Goliath
17 Prophet Zachariah
18 **Drunkenness of Noah**
19 Delphic Sibyl
20 Prophet Joel
21 **The Flood**
22 **Sacrifice of Noah**
23 Prophet Isaiah
24 Erythrean Sibyl
25 **Original Sin**
26 **Creation of Eve**
27 Cumaen Sibyl
28 Prophet Ezekiel
29 **Creation of Adam**
30 **Separation of Land from Sea**
31 Prophet Daniel
32 Persian Sibyl
33 **Creation of the Celestial Bodies and Plants**
34 **Separation of Light from Darkness**
35 Libyan Sibyl
36 Prophet Jeremiah
37 Pendentive with Brazen Serpent
38 Pendentive with Punishment of Haman
39 Prophet Jonah

Christ's ancestors

40 Lunette with Eleazar, Mathan
41 Lunette with Jacob, Joseph
42 Lunette with Azor and Sadoch
43 Lunette with Achim and Eliud
44 Lunette with Josias, Jechonias, Salathiel
45 Lunette with Zorobabel, Abiud, Eliachim
46 Lunette with Ezechias, Manasses, Amon
47 Lunette with Uzziah, Jotham, Ahaz
48 Lunette with Asa, Josaphat, Joram
49 Lunette with Roboam, Abias
50 Lunette with Jesse, David, Salomon
51 Lunette with Salomon, Booz, Obeth
52 Lunette with Naason
53 Lunette with Aminadab

Summary